Sleepless Nights

The First 42 years as an Active EMT

James W Rose

KDP Publishing

Cover Photo by John Harrington – Retired Medivac Pilot

Table of Contents

About The Author

Jim Rose has been and still is an active Emergency Medical Technician for over 42 years. His mission in life has been to help others. Thus, he has also had a great career as an educator, educational administrator, author, consultant, expert witness, and presenter in Pre-K 12 school systems and is an adjunct instructor at Columbia University. He does EMT work on a voluntary basis for the communities he has lived in, often at night when most people are sleeping. Over the years, he has been part of three volunteer fire departments with ambulances and two Volunteer Emergency Medical Ambulance companies. Jim also has a wonderful wife, who has supported and sacrificed Jim's time so that he can help others. He has two great sons who have also sacrificed Jim's time over the years. One son is also a first responder. When Jim has free time, he enjoys answering ambulance and fire calls, recreational sports, writing, and relaxing.

Jameswrose.com

James W. Rose@James_W_Rose

Photo by Nicole Whalers, EMT

Dedication

This book is dedicated to one of the first woman EMT's in the state of New York, one of the first woman Paramedics in the state of New York, and one of the first woman EMT instructors in the state of New York, my mother Lorraine Davenport. She is a true hero, not only in the EMS world, but my hero as well. It is because of her drive, her guidance and parenting that has given me the ability to be successful and led me into the world of Emergency Medical Services.

Acknowledgment

I want to acknowledge the many volunteer EMT's, paid EMT's, Paramedics, Drivers, attendants, firefighters, EMS and fire officers and police that I have worked with over the past 42 years as well as those I will work with in the future. This is truly a group of people who have sacrificed many things in their lives to help others. It is a unique group of first responders that I am honored to be part of. The list below is the organizations I have been a member of or have worked with:

Eaton's Neck Fire Department

Coram Fire department

Sayville Community Ambulance Company

Lake Carmel Fire Department

East Northport Fire Department

Huntington Community First Aid Squad

Commack Volunteer Ambulance Corps

Cold Spring Harbor Fire Department

Melville Fire Department

Dix Hills Fire Department

Commack Fire Department

Kings Park Fire Department

Selden Fire Department

Middle Island Fire Department

Gordon Heights Fire Department

Ridge Fire Department

Terryville Fire Department

Medford Fire Department

Bohemia Fire Department

Sayville Fire Department

Bayport Fired Department

West Sayville Fire Department

Holbrook Fire Department

WCMC STAT Flight

Carmel Volunteer Ambulance Corps

Eaton's Neck Coast Guard

Northport Fire Department

New York State Troopers

The National Guard

Centerport Fire Department

Greenlawn Fire Department

Carmel Fire Department

Mahopac Fire Department

Kent Fire Department

Patterson Fire Department

Pawling Fire Department

Putnam Lake Fire Department

Brewster Fire Department

North Salem Fire Department

Fishkill Fire Department

Bedford Hills Fire Department

Armonk Fire Department

White Plains Fire Department

Suffolk County Police Department

Asharoken Police Department

Carmel Police Department

Kent Police Department

In Memoriam

I want to recognize all the first responders who have put their lives on the line and are no longer with us. Two of those were my crew members for many years riding on Wednesday nights. Past Chief Robert Shannon II, who has done it all as a first responder and always had the safety of his colleagues as the first priority, and EMT Chuck Flickinger, who had saved many lives over the years.

PART I: The BEGINNING

Introduction

I was lying on the floor of a room with overturned furniture. I had an 8" knife sticking out of my abdomen. There is blood all over my shirt and on the floor around me. I was moaning in pain when the door of the room opened.

Four people walk in, and one middle-aged man comes up to me and says, "We are the …. Ambulance company."

"We are here to help you. I am an EMT. Can you tell me what happened?"

I clinch my teeth and say, "I was stabbed."

I continue to moan and slowly reach for the knife to try to pull it out, but the man grabs my arm and says, "Do not pull out the knife! We are going to stabilize it and get you to a hospital."

At the same time, another person starts moving the

furniture out of the way, while another starts checking my body for other injuries. The last person opens the med kit and starts taking out supplies to stabilize the knife.

Again, I start reaching for the knife and say, "I need this knife out." Again, the first EMT grabbed my arms, looked at the others and said, "We need one person to stay on his arms to make sure he does not pull the knife out." One crew member volunteers to hold my arms. He then grabs both arms and brings them above my head. At this point there seems to be blood on everyone. One EMT starts getting the oxygen bottle set up, while the others start trying to stabilize the knife. They begin giving me psychological first aid to help me calm down. They put a non-rebreather oxygen mask on me. This is the mask that has the highest concentration of oxygen. Once they stabilized the knife, they decided to get the scoop stretcher (this is a stretcher that divides length wise into two pieces) to bring me to the ambulance stretcher. The head EMT looks up and says, "okay, we are putting him into the ambulance," and then they all get up and walk out. The evaluator looks at me and says, "Great job Jim! What did you think?" I said, "they worked well together. They stopped me from taking the knife out. Gave me high-flow oxygen and stabilized me in a timely manner. I thought they did well." This was my initial experience with the New York State Emergency Medical System. I was about 14 years old and would do something similar to this a few times a year during the New York State Emergency Medical Technician Final Practical exam for those EMTs who needed to recertify or were taking the test for the first time. By the time I was old enough to go through the New York State Emergency Medical Technician class, I had a good understanding of what EMS was, What EMTs did, and I even knew a good portion of the knowledge and skills that you need to know to become an EMT. It was this experience that led me to becoming an EMT.

This book covers the first 42 years of the life experiences of an active volunteer Emergency Medical Technician. It is important to realize that there are EMTs all across the country that have had similar or even more intense experiences. This is the account of just one EMT as seen and remembered through his eyes. While this EMT has done thousands of calls over 42 years, only a small percentage of those calls are being relived. This book will introduce the reader to the basics of what an EMT is and how to become an EMT. Each emergency covered in this book has its own challenges, risks, and emotions that the EMTs had to deal with during the event and well after. EMTs must store the experiences they deal with and make peace with them in their own way over time. That being said, this book is therapeutic for the author as each emergency is recalled. Specific places and names of people may have been generalized or changed in order to preserve confidentiality.

Chapter One
Becoming An Emergency Medical Technician

Every state has the ability to have its own EMT certification requirements. In addition, there is a National EMT registry which can also be used as certification in many states. While things may vary from one state to another, there typically can be multiple levels of certification, such as but not limited to:

- EMT -B Basics

- AEMT-I Advanced Emergency Medical Technician Intermediate

- AEMT – CC Advanced Emergency Medical Technician Critical Care

- AEMT – P Paramedic

- The national registry involves these levels:

    o NREMT – National Registry Emergency Medical Technician

- o NRAEMT – National Registry Advanced Emergency Medical Technician

- o NRP – National Registry Paramedic

The number of hours put in a class can range from approximately 170-1800 hours, depending on the level and location of the class. To find out more about the national registry, go to nremt.org. Otherwise, you will need to look up your state's EMT requirements.

EMTs can work in a variety of capacities. This book is reviewing an EMT as a firefighter and a member of volunteer ambulance companies. Professionally, some EMTs are paid hourly in some states while others make a full salary which would depend on whether you are working for a profit company or a town or city. Even police agencies sometimes hire EMTs. No matter what you decide, whether it is paid or volunteer, the training and certification are identical.

A firefighter EMT is one who typically does first responder medical care and then transfers the patient to the ambulance. Emergency Ambulance Service handles only emergencies when they Arise. Whereas a profit ambulance organization does transports between hospitals and may be contracted to do emergency medical services for specific towns or cities.

Some areas mix both paid services and volunteer services. While this can be very challenging for a variety of reasons, often the volunteer agencies may be basic life support certified and sometimes the state or county may hire paramedic or advance life support services to supplement or support the volunteer agencies. The fact is, there is an array of opportunities around the country for Emergency Medical Technician positions. Typically, inner city environments have full-time paid EMTs and then the further you get away from the cities, the more the towns rely on volunteer organizations.

Chapter Two
"The First"

The First EMT Class

During my senior year of high school, I enrolled in my first EMT class. I remember arriving at the class and looking at all the people waiting. I was definitely the youngest at age 18, although I looked like I was 15. It appeared that many of them knew each other and had all sorts of gear that I did not have. Of course, there were a few sarcastic comments about how young I looked. Nonetheless, when the doors opened, I walked in and sat down. I was a little nervous and intimidated. The room was set up with fold-up chairs organized in rows. I chose a seat in about the third row on the right side of the room. The instructor walked out wearing a white lab-type coat. I believe she may also have been a nurse. She was overweight, round and short, about 5'2", with short black hair and glasses. She introduced herself and started talking about the expectations of the class. I believe we were also in the process of filling out some required paperwork. Once all the paperwork was completed, the instructor started teaching the class. All of a sudden! I feel some weight on my back and have two arms dangling over my shoulders. It was startling and caused me to get up and turn around. At this point, everyone in the room started moving, and the instructor started calling out orders. People were moving chairs out of the way and in a matter of seconds, there was what I refer to as a working circle around one of my classmates. It was made up of the instructor, some of her assistants and a couple of students. Orders were flying about, "Get the oxygen!" "Lie him Down!" "Maintain an Airway!" At this point, I was shocked and at the same time, I thought this was an excellent skit to start the class. I expected that everyone was going to stop and the instructor was going to talk about the reenactment for the class. But after a few minutes, I realized that it was not part of the class. The person went unconscious and fell on top of me. I did not realize this at the time, but I believe that this incident started a trend in which no matter where I was or what I was doing, the odds were that something was going to happen, which is actually covered in a later chapter called 24/7 EMT (on your own).

The First Call

It was a warm, sunny weekday during the summer of 1980. I was eighteen years old at the time. I was living in a beach community on the north shore of Long Island. I just recently received my EMT certification and was excited about the possibility of helping others in need. I just put my riding lawn mower in the garage after completing the lawn. Then it happened, the siren went off without the low-sounding whaler, which meant it was an ambulance call. I ran to my 1971 Blue Plymouth Wagon. It was my first car, with a surround sound stereo system I installed, and the car was totally shagged out. I drove my car up to the firehouse, which was only about a half mile away. When I arrived, as expected for this time of the day, we were limited in man power. I was nervous as it was my first call as an EMT and I was alone to handle the patient. The driver started the ambulance and I got in the back to start getting things together for the call. My mind was racing, not knowing what the call was going to be since, in those days, you did not get much information about the call until you showed up at the scene. The driver pulled out with the lights and sirens on and drove about a half mile to the address indicated. As I got out carrying my orange medical kit identical to the one Gage used on the Show "Emergency," I walked up to the door and rang the bell. No answer. I then knocked on the door, but again no answer. So, I opened the door and called out, "this is the ambulance. Did someone call for an ambulance?" No response. I walked in and the entrance was the living room, a 12'x12' room with two kids sitting on a couch watching TV. I looked over at the children and they just pointed to the doorway across the room. I walked across the room and into the bedroom where there was an old lady probably in her mid-70's she had gray short hair, was a little on the heavy side, and she was sitting on the end of the bed. She was staring straight ahead. I announced myself as an EMT from the fire department and asked her what her name was. Then, she started speaking Polish. I realized at this point since I do not speak Polish, that communication was going to be a problem. So, I started my primary survey. The primary survey is basically checking for major life-threatening things that affect the airway or blood flow like arterial bleeding. She was conscious, but I was not sure how alert she was, as I could not understand anything she said, but she was alert enough to talk after I said something. I moved onto my secondary survey to find out what the problem was. I noticed her eyes were unequal and one was not reactive. At this point, I was thinking that this call could be a stroke. I checked her neurological function, which showed a weakness on one side. I gave her high-flow oxygen and asked the driver to get the stretcher. We rolled the stretcher up to the bed and lifted her onto the stretcher, placing her in a sitting position. We put her into the ambulance and I got in the back to switch her to the onboard oxygen and started to prepare for the long forty-minute ride to the hospital. At this time, I was glad I made it through my first scene, but I was concerned about the long trip. My mind was racing again, what if she goes into cardiac arrest? I started to complete my vitals during the drive. I thank God that my first call was what I call a textbook stroke, meaning it was easy to identify because it followed exactly what was taught in our class. However, most calls are not that easy as I found out over the years. We did get her to the hospital alive and stable, considering she was a stroke patient. Now, when I was trained, the first thing they told us was, you pick the patient up, get them to the hospital and then forget about it. Do not follow up on every call, or you will not be able to do this job for that long. So, I never heard anything after dropping her off at the hospital.

I was feeling very good after that call, I felt that I had helped save her life and that being an Emergency Medical Technician does make a difference. I learned that despite the unique challenges like the patient speaking Polish and having no crew members, that I can still achieve the goal. I never thought at that time that my entire life would be devoted towards helping others, I just knew it was the right thing to do for this small beach community.

PART II: CALLS RECALLED FROM MULTIPLE AGENCIES

Chapter Three

Assaults

There are many different types of assaults that can take place, from simple fist-fighting to shootings and stabbings. For this chapter I will cover a few assault calls that stand out in my mind. Shootings will be covered in chapter six.

One of the first things an EMT must do when arriving at a scene is to make sure the scene is safe. This is even more important in an assault situation. When I first started as an EMT, police were not available and often did not show up for calls. Now a days, where I currently practice, police are often called to the scene and for a known violence call, they are called to the scene first to make sure the scene is secured. When this happens, we are told to have our ambulance stage away, which means to park in a safe location so that we are not in the scene area and will not become part of the scene. Then you wait. Waiting can take a few minutes or much longer, depending on the scenario.

I remember one call many years ago in the mid-1980s. The call came over the pager as a head injury. It was late at night, so it was dark outside and rather cool. When we arrived at the scene, it was just me and a driver. When I walked into the house, I saw a woman sitting in a chair at a table in the dining room. She looked like she was in her 60's. She had short, straight gray hair and on the right side of her head had a huge lump the size of a baseball. She was conscious but not coherent. While, I was surveying her injuries, I found that she was unable to answer any questions as to what happened. I started looking around the room for some clues. I did not see anything knocked over or disturbed, which made me think she did not have a fall. As my partner walked in, so did her husband from another room. The husband also had gray hair, looked like he was in his 60s and was in good shape probably, about 6'2." He appeared to be anxious. When my partner came in, my partner closed the door, and behind the door was a baseball bat. At this point, I eyed my partner to look behind the door, so that he knew the potential situation. When you ride enough with people, you learn to signal or read each other's body language so that you do not cause a disturbance that can escalate a scene. At that point, he turned around and walked out and called for police back up, and then returned with the stretcher. Now, our goals are to be able to keep everything as calm as possible and to make sure the husband does not get near the bat behind the door. I started asking the husband questions about his wife, does she have any medical conditions? Is she allergic to anything? And if he knew how this happened? He said, "She fell," which just did not match any of the injuries I was seeing and as I stated earlier, there were no other signs in the room of a fall. At this point, the husband started pacing and it was very obvious he was becoming more and more distraught. A few minutes later, the police arrived at the door. When the police came in, the husband began to be more anxious, "why are the police here!!" He yelled. I said sir, it is normal procedure to have police arrive at an emergency scene to see if they can assist in anyway. Now, I looked at the police officer and told him she apparently had a fall, while I was eyeing the area behind the door to the police officer. Whenever you are in an atmosphere that can become dangerous, it is always nice to see our friends in blue arrive at the scene. This was definitely one of those moments. When the police started questioning the husband again, the husband became very agitated. This progressively got worse as the questions became more and more targeted. It was at this time that we loaded the patient onto the stretcher and took her out of the house loading her into the ambulance. I am not sure what the police decided and what the outcome was for the husband, but we did get the woman to the hospital for further evaluation of a head injury. Unfortunately, she was still incoherent when we transferred her over to the nurses at the hospital.

There was another night that stands out to me as well. It was also in the mid-1980s. It was a warm summer night and the tones announced a stabbing at a local bar on the main roadway, which goes through many towns on Long Island. When we arrived at this bar scene, our senses were peaking, trying to pick up on any dangers as we approached the patient. The police were not present at the time and bar scenes can be very tricky because you tend to have a lot of people who are emotional about whatever occurred and not very rational in their thoughts. So, as we walked into the bar, it was crowded with people standing shoulder to shoulder with one exception as there was a circle around the patient. We are looking at all the individuals to see if anyone stands out or if anyone has a weapon or something that can be used as a weapon. When I reach the victim, my first question to anyone in the room is if they know where to attacker is? They said he left right after the attack. You also do not want to stay on this type of scene very long for many reasons. First, you always want to remember the golden hour, (basically, the data shows that getting the patient to the hospital within an hour increases the chances of saving them or correcting the situation). In addition, attackers often come back to the scene, especially at bar scenes where the person is likely drunk. So, the faster we work the better for all involved. In this case, it was a straight puncture wound to the abdominal region. We dressed and bandaged the victim and put him in the ambulance. The police arrived just as we were leaving. We took the person to our nearest trauma center. Right after we dropped off the patient, we received another call on the same road at another bar a little further east from the bar we were just at. It came over as another stabbing. We responded from the hospital and when we arrived at the scene, it was almost identical to the last call. Again, we were told the attacker left the area. Fortunately, in this town, the trauma center was only about twenty minutes away. Again, just as we were leaving the hospital, we received another call and another stabbing at a bar just east of the last call. We are now noticing a pattern rather than a coincidence. So, we repeated everything for a third time. We were wondering and actually expecting a possibility of a fourth call, but we realized that if it follows the pattern, we are seeing, the next bar was in the next town. Thus, not our jurisdiction. We had heard later that there was a call in the next town and that the police did catch the attacker.

Chapter Four
Fires

Fires can produce many victims depending on the type of fire and how out of control it gets. Often, the ambulance's response to a fire is to give support to the firefighters who are putting their lives on the line to save the house and people that may be in it. We are there if something goes wrong or fire fighters rescue a person. So, as we approach the fire, we need to consider what type of fire we are going to? If it is a house fire, we could have patients pulled out or a firefighter could get hurt. It could be a brush fire, car fire or even a campfire that is out of control. I remember one day many years ago in the 1980's when we were called to a house fire in the town just south of my district. It was a day fire during the summer evening. We did not have a good response to the ambulance, as it was me and one driver. When I approach a fire scene, I start reviewing in my head the protocols which commonly change over time or could be locally different then the last place I rode for. We arrived at the scene at about the same time as the fire trucks. You could see this two-story white house with flames coming out of the roof and windows. It was considered a "working structure fire." As we got closer, it appeared that someone was throwing something out of a second-story window. It was hard to tell exactly what was happening, I said to the driver, "Look at that! What is being thrown out of the window?" The driver was not sure, but when the second one was thrown out and I was a little closer I was able to see that it was a black female throwing out a small white package. I said, "I think she is throwing out babies wrapped in blankets?" Once we got close enough, I ran over to the area where the packages landed. There were shrubs under the window, which I believe she was aiming for, as I found that she was throwing out her children wrapped in a blanket. Because they were still close to the raging fire and it was very hot, I grabbed the three children wrapped up and took them to the ambulance. It was three babies ranging from about a month old to about 21 months old. I opened all of the blankets and started three oxygen lines to set up for blow-by-oxygen. When an infant needs oxygen, you do not want to give too much as it can harm them, so you use the blow-by method by having the oxygen blown pass their face. I then surveyed all the babies to see what injuries they had. Fortunately, they only had scrapes and bruises, so the main concern was whether they had smoke inhalation damage or internal injuries. Although they did not seem to have any signs of this, it was a two-story drop. I believe the shrubs and blanket limited the impact. Once I stabilized each child, we then took the children to the hospital. I always wondered, what happened to the mother in that fire? Did the fireman get to her? Was she alright? She saved her babies that day. She is a true hero in my mind.

Sometimes, you are called to a large-scale or ongoing fire where you again are needed to give support to those working the fire. For example, a couple of years ago, we had a large brush fire, which eventually became more of a brush dump fire that went on for weeks. Firefighters would be there all day and all night fighting the fire. Eventually, taking shifts to contain the fire because the fire was so deep with brush that it just was not going out. The chief had to call in bulldozers to try to help. Eventually, the brush piled up in this pit had to be removed and trucked out. As an EMT on the ambulance at this type of event, you are making sure all the firefighters are hydrated and handling any injuries that may occur as they come up.

Chapter Five
Overdoses

Overdoses can be very challenging and sometimes the most dangerous types of calls. As an EMT in a Long Island beach community during the 1980, we had a good amount of overdose calls. At the time, angel dust, heroin, and marijuana were very popular. We had one facility that kept us busy with overdose calls, where we would often get calls for young males on angel dust. This drug, otherwise known as PCP, is a hallucinogen that can cause violent behavior coupled with superhuman strength. So, during my younger years, when we did not have police at the scenes, and did not get information about the call-in advance and did not have the readily available drug antidotes like Narcan, we were stuck going to scenes to save people who at the time of the incident did not want saving. So, I could not count the number of times I had to wrestle with someone under the influence of drugs.

One time, we received a call in this town, which at

the time used sirens to notify first responders around the town. I like the town sirens; I believe they were much more efficient and also let the community know there was an emergency and that first responders would be getting into their vehicles and responding. In this town, when the sirens went off, the entire town got off the streets and stopped what they were doing to allow the first responders to respond. Basically, everyone would step off the streets, whether they were walking, playing, or riding a bike. So, I got into my car and went to the firehouse.

When we got to the firehouse, the address was given to us. We knew because this facility had many drug overdoses that, we thought we were walking into another overdose. We had a full crew of four and a fire truck with more manpower if needed. The patient was a white male approximately 6' tall, about 160 pounds and in good physical shape. As we arrived, we could hear him screaming at everyone around him. We walked up to him, trying to calm him down, but quickly lost him to hallucinations as he started throwing everything in the room. At one point, we had 6 people on him, two on each arm and two across the legs. In this particular case, all of us were pretty good size except for me, who at the time was about 95 pounds. What helped me was that I had an extensive wrestling background. When we thought we had him with the six guys on top of him, it did not last long. In fact, with ease, this man just lifted one arm, throwing the two men across the room. Then he lifted the arm I was on with a fireman, throwing the two of us across the room. So, it took us a long while to be able to control the situation and get him on the stretcher and into the ambulance.

Dealing with patients who abused opioids was also fairly popular as well. However, with these patients it was a totally different experience. Often, the people who overdosed using these drugs became unconscious and died. We did not usually wrestle with these addicts; we just tried to keep them alive. I remember one call where he thought he was being attacked by spiders and kept trying to get them off. However, of course, there weren't any spiders. Sometimes, trying to join their world can temporarily get them on the stretcher. Today, at least with opioids, you have a drug that can counteract the overdose. Narcan to me, is somewhat of a miracle drug for this situation. Recently, I was on a call where we arrived second on the scene. When I walked up to the patient, the medic said, he had given this comatose patient two Narcan doses so far, but he is not seeing any change. He then asked me to give him another dose. I was just about to give him the Narcan when, all of a sudden, he woke up. Problem solved, time to transport to the nearest hospital.

Chapter Six
Shootings

Shooting injuries are very traumatic and vary depending on the part of the body shot and the type of gun being used. Unfortunately, while I have done my share of shooting calls, I believe gun violence will continue to get worse as mass shootings continue to shock this country on a regular basis. I am only one EMT with 42 years of experience, but it is my opinion that a majority of shootings that I have arrived at would not have taken place if the gun was not easily accessed. A common shooting is during a suicide, which will be covered in chapter eleven.

Some shooting calls that standout to me took place in the mid-1980s. My tones went off at about ten o'clock one summer night. It was toned out as a shooting victim on the side of the road. As we approached the area, we started looking for signs that the shooter may still be around. We did not see anyone in the area except for a person sitting on the side of the road. He was a man, who was about 25 years old, had short brown hair and was in good shape wearing shorts. He was holding his lower right leg. I introduced myself as an EMT with the fire department and asked him what happened. He said, "I was walking down the street and I heard a pop and then had a burning in my leg, I think I was shot." Upon my evaluation, he seems to have an entrance wound without an exit wound. I dressed and bandaged the leg and we quickly loaded him into the ambulance in case the shooter was still in the area. We left the scene and I then completed a full secondary survey to find the only wound being the one gunshot wound to his leg. We took him to the nearby trauma center.

About a week later, I had a similar call, but this time, the person was shot in the arm and said he thought it came from a passing car. Again, I dressed and bandaged the arm and took him to the trauma center. Another week or so later, I was toned out again for another shooting victim on the side of the road. Now, at this point I am seeing a pattern. Fortunately, all the calls I made from this shooter, if it was one person, were not too serious. I am not sure how many other shootings took place on other shifts, but I do know that the side road shootings did take place for about two to three months and then stopped. I am assuming that the police caught the shooter.

One shooting that occurred in the late 1980s after midnight, sent us to a main road of this town, but when we arrived, the road was blocked by police. They waved us into the scene which was in the middle of the road which in this area was lined with woods. The patient was a middle-aged man with a gun shot to the chest. As we were evaluating him, a police officer came over to us and said we just got word that the shooter is in the woods, which was about ten feet from us. Okay, now it is time to scoop and go. We quickly loaded him onto the stretcher and put him in the ambulance. We then drove the ambulance about a mile away so we can be assured that we were in a safe location. then we dressed and bandaged the wound for our trip. Fortunately, the hole did not have an exit wound and was not a sucking chest wound, which is when hole actually affects the lung cavity in which the lungs suck in air through the hole. In that case we would have needed to seal the hole with saran wrap. However, this was a basic dress bandage and go. We dropped our patient off at our trauma center still alive.

Chapter Seven
Motor Vehicle Accidents

Motor Vehicle Accidents keep emergency ambulances busy. You never know what to expect when you arrive at the scene of an MVA. Some jurisdictions refer to them as Personal Injury Auto Accidents or PIAA. Years ago, in the mid-1980s, I had ridden Friday night shifts, which were very busy later in the night due to the fact that drivers would leave the bars and get into accidents. Since that time in New York, the drinking laws have changed from 18 years of age to 21 years of age, and then the cars' safety requirements improved. Often, these were the calls we needed to call a helicopter for. I have probably dealt with thousands of MVAs over the years.

Years ago, when I was a young EMT with about five years of experience, I lived in a town that had two four-lane intersecting roadways. We often had MVA's at this intersection and were the only ambulance for multiple patients. In this location, when we showed up at the scene, we usually had patients all over and quite a distance away from each other. I remember one call where we came to this intersection, and I was riding with a man who I will refer to as Tom, he had severe asthma and was more experienced and older than I. When we got out, we saw three victims scattered about; we walked over to the closest victim and Tom jumped into action. He was the fastest and probably the best-skilled EMT I have ever seen. He literally had the patient surveyed and packaged in no time and then moved on to the next patient. To this day, I have never seen anyone like this man. He was just amazing. Not only was he fast, precise and skilled, but he was doing all of these while coughing and wheezing from severe asthma. I thought he was going to be the next patient.

The trickiest part of this intersection was that the cars were always going so fast that the accidents were spread out, sometimes like a ¼ mile away. In this district, we had about 2800 calls with only six active EMTs. It was a very busy district and we were often handling multiple patients. The general rule is to try to have car accident victims separated on different ambulances so they do not start a fight on the way to the hospital. Sometimes that is not an option.

Probably one of the worst accidents I have been involved with occurred in 1997, when a driver was coming off an interstate and ran into an illegally parked tractor-trailer. It was estimated that he hit the back of the tractor-trailer at about 65 miles per hour. This took place at about 2:30 AM. I was the first one to the car once we got on the scene. When I walked up, I noticed a bunch of metal crunched up underneath the tractor-trailer. This was a wagon that, at this point, was crunched up to about a 6' heap of metal. I was not able to see a patient when I opened what was left of the door. It was very dark and the fire truck with lighting had not arrived yet. While I was looking, I noticed a body deep under the dashboard area. The body was curled up in a small ball. The person was screaming in pain, which I took as a good sign considering the condition of the car. When the trucks arrived and the

Chief was on the scene, I asked if we could get a helicopter for this patient, knowing that there appeared to be massive injuries and I am not sure how long it will take us to get the person out of the car.

As mentioned earlier, the golden hour will be crucial during this call. Because the victim was under the dashboard, it may take time to lift the dashboard so we can get the patient out. While I was checking the patient to see what we were dealing with, I noticed the dashboard was impaled with tools. There were multiple screwdrivers and a small saw. It was like the tools were shot into a target. I am not sure if it was one of the tools or something else in the car that triggered my memory, I thought, I know this car! I looked around and realized it was my neighbor, a friend that I will refer to as Ted. I said, "Ted, is that you?" He replied, "Jim!" I said, "yes Ted, we are going to get you out of here." A few minutes later we were able to pull him out from underneath the dashboard, from underneath the tractor trailer, and we began to work on him. He had a bad head injury, a fractured hip, multiple lacerations and likely internal injuries. We were able to package him and then the helicopter arrived and we put him on the helicopter, which took him to the trauma center. A call like this involves many people working together, you have the Chief coordinating the scene and calling the helicopter and making sure we have a landing zone, you have the police and fire police closing down the road and dealing with the traffic issues. The firefighters were making sure the scene remained safe and cutting the patient out of the car. The ambulance staff and/or firefighter Emt's helping with the patient. And, of course, you have the helicopter crew and the medics and nurses on board.

In this case, it was a neighbor and a friend I had worked on and now I am not sure if he would survive the flight to the trauma center, and if he did, I wasn't sure he would live long in the hospital. Once he flew off, I told the Chief that he was a friend and that I needed to tell his wife what had happened. The Chief gave me permission to leave the scene. Now, I was dealing with an area I had never dealt with before. How do you tell a friend that her husband was just in a bad accident and we flew him down to a trauma center that is about forty-five minutes away by car and that I am not sure if he will survive? I was trying to control my emotions, which seemed to be much easier at the scene. It was now about 3:30 AM, I knocked on the door and there wasn't an answer. I rang the bell and knocked again. His wife finally answered. She said, "Jim what are you doing here?" I explained that Ted had been in an accident and I needed to take her down to the trauma center right away. We made quick arrangements for someone to come over to watch the kids who were sleeping and we got in my car and drove down to the hospital. I can honestly say it was one of the longest drives of my life. She was very upset and had a lot of questions. I did not want her to get her hopes up because I truly was not sure he was going to be alive when we arrived. So, I told her the details of the accident and the obvious injuries I dealt with and let her know there could be internal injuries. It was a long day and turned into a long week, but Ted is still walking around today. Although, he has some scars and a limp. I have since lost touch with Ted, but I occasionally see his now ex-wife at parties when she comes back to town to visit.

Motor vehicles can have an accident with many other things, such as a house, a deer, or even a person. One time, at the same major intersection mentioned previously, for the massive accidents, we had a call for a motor vehicle vs. a pedestrian. On the way to the call, I knew that this was likely going to be bad because of the speed that cars travel at this intersection. We had a crew of four, including my wife, who had just become an EMT. In this particular town you were thrown into some of the worst situations for a new EMT. When we got to the scene on this rainy day, we saw sneakers on the roadway next to the car at the point of impact and a man who looked homeless lying in the roadway about 75' away. Evidently, he was hit at such high speeds that it blew him out of his shoes. When I walked up to him, I noticed the critical nature of this call. He was unconscious, had a huge lump on the front right side of his head, had many lacerations, and a broken right femur. His vitals were not good, we knew we had to work fast. The first step was having one of us maintain an airway and putting him on high-flow oxygen so that he could breathe. The next step was to put a traction splint on. As a new EMT, this was a lot for my wife, I was glad we had a full crew. My wife did a great job as she did most of the work putting on the Hare Traction. The man had not showered in a long time and the smell was strong. We were fortunate to be only about fifteen minutes from the trauma center. Which I believe we made in ten minutes. We not only maintained the airway, but we actually had to breath for this patient as he was carrying out a slow set of chain stokes breathing, which is a rhythmic breathing pattern that can occur with severe head injuries. We also took care of many open wounds and figured there were internal injuries as well. When we transferred him to the trauma center that day, he was alive. I am not sure if he survived over the next few days. At the end of this call, I thought we had done everything we could and I was particularly proud of my wife for stepping up as a brand-new EMT. After a call like this, the ambulance is a mess with blood everywhere, gauze, tape, medical supplies scattered, and pieces of clothing here and there. It can take longer to clean the ambulance then it took to complete the call.

About ten to twelve years ago, we were called to a scene of a motor vehicle accident, where a car crashed into a telephone pole. Cars into large trees and/or telephone poles usually do not have good results. In this case, the car slid sideways, hitting the telephone pole with the passenger front door. The only positive thing about this call was that there wasn't anyone in the passenger seat. As I walked up to the car, the first thing I checked was the pole itself and the wires to make sure everything was still intact. In this case, the pole was damaged, but everything was still intact. So, I walked up to the car, and the window was open. There was hard rock music blasting very loudly. The driver was unconscious but breathing, with blood coming out of his mouth. I reached over and turned the music off, so I could think and also hear our rescuers as we worked on the patient. When I did a secondary assessment, I did not see any other signs of injury, but estimated from the damage to the car that this car was moving at a very high speed. There was also blood coming from his left ear, which could also mean a possible skull fracture.

The driver was not wearing a seat belt and was actually in the middle of the long front seat, which was right next to the pole. Since he had blood coming out of his mouth and ear, I also suspected that there were other internal injuries as well. I looked over to the Chief and asked for a helicopter. The landing zone was set up at a nearby school. We put a collar on the patient to stabilize his neck and removed him from the wreckage with a backboard. We then put him in the ambulance and put him on high-flow oxygen, started taking his vitals and because his respirations were so low, we had to bag him (breath for him) and suction the blood out of his mouth between respirations. The helicopter arrived about ten minutes later, and we transferred care to the staff in the helicopter. I am not sure if he survived the trip down to the trauma center. I knew his chances were not all that good at the time.

One night not too long ago, my crew and I were just finishing up a call at the local hospital when our tones went off for a motor vehicle accident at a summer camp at the northeast end of our district. The tones went off asking for two ambulances at a summer camp, which was not open since school had already started for the year. Much of the roads back there are dirt and one wonders why someone would be driving back there at this point in time, not to mention actually going fast enough to get into an accident. Nevertheless, we reported on our radio that we were en route. It is a long drive from the hospital to this location, so I figured we were not going to be there first. Once we made the last turn and started to see the scene from a distance, we saw a great deal of emergency lights. Typically, you would have maybe a fire engine, fire Chief, ambulance, a police car, and a medic car, but what we were seeing was much more than that.

As we got closer, I counted about ten state trooper cars plus all the rescue vehicles, such as a fire truck, a Chief's car, an ambulance, and a medic car. Something else was going on here. We pulled up to the scene and I asked the Chief where he wanted us. This was a thin, tared very narrow road. The Chief said, "pull up there, the car that crashed is right here," as he pointed to the side of the road just behind him, "the patients all ran up there," as he pointed down the road. So my partner and I got out of the ambulance and the driver stayed with the rig. We came up to the first state trooper's car and an officer said, "one is in here," pointing to the back seat of the car." The mother and kids are up ways, "and there is one more way up there that the other ambulance is taking care of." I looked at my partner, who was also an EMT, and asked what car she wanted to go to, she said, "I want mom and the kids," I said, "Okay, I will take this one." It was very difficult to see since it was about 8 PM in the woods with no lights on the side of the road and a great deal of emergency lights flickering. It gave a strobe kind of appearance you almost wanted to disco, but I contained myself and looked into the car.

The state trooper assigned to this patient asked if I

needed light and I said, "that would be great." You never know what you are getting into when dealing with someone in the back seat of a police car. Sometimes, the police are being nice and give a person a place to sit, other times, they are in custody or being investigated and may be in custody soon, but I still did not have any information. When I bent over and the officer shined the light in the back, I saw a young skinny black man probably in his late 20's. He was cuffed which gives me some idea of what happened, but still did not have the full story. I introduced myself and asked if he had any pain anywhere. He was talking very low and he was not very coherent. His words were not very clear. He said his left leg and right side hurt. He was sitting with his back to me and his leg up on the seat away from me.

My first thought, seeing the cuffs were that this was likely a drunk driving accident. I then told the officer I needed to make access to the victim on the other side so I could check out his leg. He said no problem. Even though the man was cuffed, we still did not have any story as to why, I did not know how dangerous this situation was and only knew that the man did run from the police after the crash. Often, when we have to treat a cuffed patient, they seem to want to delay the process of being arrested and possibly tested. Therefore, they often have pain and want to go to the hospital.

I opened the door and told him I would be checking his leg, as soon as I barely touched it, he went through the roof with pain. It was an Academy Award performance. I said, "I barely touched you." He said, "it hurt really bad." I said, "okay, then I will need to cut your pants so I can take a better look at it." He gave me permission and screamed in pain the entire time I cut his sweatpants up about six inches. I got my emergency deluxe pen light out which was an LED light that folded and lit up in multiple ways. It was a good light for this situation. I used the long light initially, which was about 2 inches long and pretty bright. I set it up on the seat so I could see what I was looking at. My evaluation found two small abrasions on his shin, no deformity, and no loss of motor function. But

I always give the patient the benefit of the doubt, so I thought I would use the Frac Pac as a precaution in case there was an X-ray fracture, which is a fracture you cannot see without an X-ray. Then I said, "I need to check your ribs," and he said, "okay," and screamed in pain again, but not as loudly. He said, "it hurts but not as bad as the leg." I then got out and asked the police officer how he got into the car. He said this was a police chase that started on one highway on the west side of the county, went up to the interstate in the next county and came east to our county again, getting off at our exit. He said, "they drove in here, hit the tree and they got out and started running. So once we got him after the chase, we walked him over here." So, it confirmed that it was likely not a bad break since he could run on it and there wasn't any deformity.

Now, as to why this all happened and why this man who was the driver would risk his family in a police chase is one thing I wondered about. As I continued the assessment, I found no other injuries, but his eyes were pinpointed in a dark environment, so he was on a drug. I asked if he took any medication and he said no. So that means it was likely an illegal substance that was causing his pinpoint pupils and slurred speech. If I had to choose, it was probably a narcotic of some type, such as but not limited to heroin, morphine, or fentanyl. Since we are presently dealing with a heroin epidemic again similar to the 80s, I would guess that it is possible that this is the drug of choice. As I was working on the driver of the crashed car, my partner walked by with a parade of babies and a mother as they headed toward the ambulance. The Chief came over shortly and said that I will stay with my patient and hand the patient off to the third ambulance that was coming from a neighboring town in the next county.

Now, the medical officer in charge of the scene is from the next town and he is trying to figure out where all the patients will be going. So there were three ambulances one was going south to the county below our county to the level one trauma center, with three babies and a mother. And the patient I was working on is going north to the next county up to another trauma center. The third is also going north, but to another hospital altogether from what I was told. I was also told that the chase ended with all the crash victims running into the woods where the parents were hiding the babies. So, the police had to chase them down and then find all the babies. Hence, the many state trooper cars that are at the scene. Each ambulance is assigned a state trooper who will escort the ambulance to the hospital as they were all arrested in cuffs, and they did not believe there was much of a threat or they would have put a trooper in the rig with the first responders taking care of the patients. This call took many hours of work to actually complete everything and get the ambulance ready for the next call. My partner had it the worst as she had three reports that had to be completed when we got back from the long drive to the trauma center. The golden hour was not achieved and was not necessarily needed. If any of the patients were actually really hurt badly, we would have flown them to the trauma center to stay under the golden hour. Just another sleepless night for many volunteer first responders.

About twenty years ago, when I was a member of a private volunteer ambulance company, the tones went off for a call as a motorcycle accident on a roadway. It was during the day; I believe it was a cool fall day and we only had three of us that showed up for the call. When we arrived at the location, we saw a person with a quad type of vehicle standing on the side of the road. We got out and asked if he had been in an accident, and he said, "no, the accident was in the woods pretty far in and my friend is not in good shape." So we grabbed the radios and some equipment, I believe we took a backboard, trauma bag, oxygen, and jumped on the quad, leaving our driver with the ambulance. This was before ALS (Advanced Life Support) was available in this area of the state. We were riding into a heavily wooded area. He took us into the woods about a mile to an area where motorcyclists did motocross.

As we approached the area, we could see dirt trails and hear other motorcycles. This was not an organized motocross trail, but one that appears to be used by the local teenagers. On the side of one of the trails, we saw a motorcycle down and a person lying next to the motorcycle with a couple of others near him. I asked what happen and they said he was going over the trail and just lost control and crashed. He did not hit a tree, but as often happens with this type of accident, if you do not hit an object that will do the damage, then it will be the actual road or motorcycle itself that does the damage.

He was lying on his back in pain with an obvious laceration in the abdominal area, as I could see the shirt covered in blood. Upon the secondary survey, we found that he had about a 12" laceration across the abdominal area in a u shape. I looked at the bike and noticed the footrest was a metal piece that had lost its rubber and had sharp edges. At that time, I thought that perhaps when he was tumbling with the bike, the footrest opened up his stomach. The wound was very deep, but fortunately, the bowels seemed to be still intact and were not protruding. He had a few other minor lacerations and a possible dislocated shoulder. My partner stabilized the shoulder and I bandaged the open wound on the stomach, which called for a large trauma dressing with foil over the top to keep the area warm. The teenager was in a lot of pain mostly in the stomach. We asked if his parents were notified and they said not yet, we wanted to get you guys first.

At that point, a police officer arrived on the scene on foot. We informed him that the parent needed to be contacted and he radioed his dispatch to try to locate the parent. This was well before cell phones were popular. Once we stabilized the teen, we put him on 15 liters of oxygen via a non-rebreather, which is a face mask with a bag under it. Probably one of the most common delivery tools for oxygen, especially because it delivers high concentration at a high flow rate, which is called for during traumatic accidents. We put him on a backboard with plenty of straps as we knew it was going to be a very bumpy ride back to the road. We knew we had to move quick because it took time to get to him and the golden hour was ticking away. Since it was daytime and very few volunteers were available and since time was of the essence, we decided to take the victim out that same we came in. We told the teen to take it very slow for us so we did not lose his friend off the back of the quad.

We got on placing the board on the back and fastening it to the quad, which obviously was not designed for this type of action. We both climbed on board and held the board in place, making sure that everything remained stable. The teen did a great job navigating the bumps and keeping a slow and steady speed. When we came out of the woods, his mother was there with our driver. We explained the condition of her child to her and said we needed to get him to the hospital. She was okay with it and actually road in the front of the ambulance. We were only about 12 minutes from the hospital and we arrived with a conscious child with a severe open stomach wound, multiple cuts and abrasions and a possible dislocated shoulder. I expected that he would be on his feet in a day or two and hopefully have a full recovery.

Chapter Eight
Weather Related Emergencies

Hurricanes

I have been in a fair number of hurricanes over the years. The one that stands out most to me is Hurricane Gloria. I was volunteering on Long Island at the time. Everyone felt ready to handle the hurricane and as per normal protocol, we were called to stand by at the firehouse. I vividly remember standing at the firehouse, looking out the windows of the garage doors. You can hear the wind blowing and whistling and the sounds of crashing. Then, all of a sudden, I am watching these huge oak trees blowing by the firehouse like match sticks in the wind. It was like slow motion, watching these trees just lift off the ground and glide until they hit the McDonalds nearby. They came one at a time, like a parade and all ended up in the same place.

After sometime, our first call came in. Everyone was anxious not only were we going to a call, but we were concerned about our safety in just getting to the call. We turned left out of the firehouse and then took another left down the next road. Once we made the turn, the driver stopped. There were many trees down across the road, and this was the only viable way to get to the location of the call. We called for our rescue truck, which responded and started cutting and moving all the trees so we could continue the call. It took about 40 minutes to get the road cleared enough to get the ambulance through. Fortunately, the call was minor.

Ice Conditions

The one thing I learned over the years is that there is a point in time where all the conditions come together to make all hell break loose on an interstate highway. Sometimes, it is dense fog and other times, it is icing. The dense fog is dangerous because drivers may not be aware that they are driving into it and even worse, if there are other cars and trucks that already found out. You are just driving along and then it whites out you cannot see a foot in front of you. By the time you try to slow down, you have run into the chain of vehicles before you. Fortunately, I have not dealt with this crisis firsthand. However, the other is when in a split-second, everything freezes on the road. It is like an instant ice rink for any vehicle moving. I have dealt with this scenario on a number of occasions.

One time we received our tones for a motor vehicle accident on the interstate. I got into my car to go to the firehouse, which was slow and difficult. I finally got to the firehouse. There were only two of us at the time. The ambulance driver drove us to the interstate. Once we got on the interstate all you could see was cars scattered everywhere in every direction. We knew the location of our call and continued monitoring everything we saw and calling into dispatch what we were finding. We started getting close to our call location and came to a hill. It was not a steep hill, but it was impossible to go up. We believe we saw the accident we were looking for, so we decided to see if we could walk the rest of the way since nothing was moving on the highway it was virtually closed. When we got out, we could not stand much less walk up the hill to the waiting patient. We made the decision to get a longboard, put the med kit on the board and then try to go up the hill on our bellies to get to the car. We had one person in the front and the other in the back, each holding the board as we scurried up the roadway on our stomachs.

Eventually, after about six minutes of fighting the hill, we made it to the car. The patient had pain in the neck, and back as well as one of his legs. We secured the patient to the backboard and then with one of us sitting in the front and one of us sitting in the back, we slid down the hill, trying to make sure we did not pick up too much speed. We made it back to the ambulance and got the patient inside. We then turned around going back out the same way we came in. We decided that the back roads were more passible and took the back roads to the nearest hospital.

Chapter Nine
Medical Emergencies

Medical calls are probably the most common calls we do and the most routine calls as well. Basically, you arrive at the scene, make sure the person is breathing and is conscious and then you ask what the problem is and you start trying to solve the mystery. Sometimes, it is easy to figure out, like the First call I ever did in the chapter noted as "The First," and other times it is much more difficult. I will never forget my first heart attack call, which took place in that beautiful beach community I grew up in. It was at a house in a wooded area where the houses were known for their size and amount of land. We had a full crew of four. It was in an evening, I believe, in the fall or possibly the summer. We had a driver, my mother as one of the paramedics, another man we will call Bill, also a paramedic, and me a new EMT. If you have ever seen the show "Emergency," this scene looked identical to the scenes on that show.

In those days, paramedics had to have the

medication read three times before giving it as to make sure there weren't any mistakes. So, my mother established an IV took out the medication and read the package out loud, then passed it to me and I read it out loud and then Bill read it out loud. Then, it was passed to my mother, who administered it. Advanced Life Support was very new to our area but also very important because we were so far from a hospital. It was nice to be able to ride with a set of new paramedics (AEMTs) since it was so new to the area. En-route to the hospital, our patient did improve mostly due to the care given by the AEMTs.

In the same community many years ago, the sirens went off and I drove to the fire house with my blue light on my blue Plymouth Wagon. Once I arrived, I was the first, so I had to call dispatch to get the location of the call. Then a driver arrived so we got into the ambulance and went to the location. This was back in the early to mid-1980s before OSHA mandated EMTs to wear gloves. We arrived at this two-story small cape with brown shingles. I picked up our bright orange medical kit and I walked to the door. I rang the bell, but no answer. So, I then knocked on the door, but still no answer. Then I tried to open the door, but it was locked. So, I walked over to a window to see if I could see anything helpful, and I saw an elderly lady who appeared to be unconscious lying on her back. She had gray hair, was fully dressed, and was possibly in her 80s. I looked over at my driver and said, "I see an unconscious woman on the floor, but the door is locked." We have to get in there!" The driver replied, "I will see if there is a back door that is open." He went around to the left of the house and I walked around to see if possibly there was another route of entrance, such as an open window. When I got to the back, the driver yelled over. "The back door is open!" So, we went into the house through the back door. We walked through the kitchen and into the living room, where the lady was on the floor. I said, "Mam, we are the ambulance. Do you need help?" No answer, I got down on my knees, leaned over, put my face near her face, and looked, listened and felt, otherwise known as evaluating the ABCs (Airway, breathing, and circulation). When you do this, you are looking to see if there is a chest rise or any major bleed, then you are seeing if you feel any air exchange on your cheek, at the same time feeling for the carotid pulse and listening for air exchange. She was breathing, did not have any major bleeds, had a pulse, and I also noticed other things, such as her skin conditioning, which was normal color and at a normal temperature. I said to the driver, "Let's use the scoop stretcher," so the driver went out to get the stretcher and I started the secondary survey, looking for other clues as to why this person was unconscious. The driver came back with the scoop stretcher, which is the stretcher that divides in half so you can put it on without a lot of movement of the patient. I put the stretcher down next to the patient and adjusted the length to match her size. Then, I unlocked the latch at each end to separate the stretcher into equal halves of the same length, I put one-half next to her on each side, making sure that I walked around her and did not pass anything over her. A luxury, we had because of her location. Because of her size, we were going to need to slightly roll her and lift her clothes out of the way. So, I reached under her and got a surprise, she had apparently urinated and everything I was touching was soaked and she was lying in it as it was on the hardwood floor. So, now my hands were covered in urine and I began adjusting her so we could lock the stretch under her. We got the two pieces close enough to lock and I locked the device so we could pick her up and move her to the ambulance stretcher. Once we got her into the ambulance, I was able to unlock the scoop and remove it. We went lights and sirens to the nearest hospital about forty minutes away. When working on an unconscious person, you basically make sure the airway is secured, so I put in an oral airway, and then put her on oxygen and then started taking the vital signs (respirations, pulse, eye reaction, skin condition, and blood pressure) during the primary survey that I did in the house, the idea was to just make sure all these necessities were actually working.

Now, it is time to see how well they are working by counting and checking for quality. So, after I completed this step, I determined that we had an unconscious woman in her 80s who had stable vitals. Vital signs should be done every few minutes so you can see if there is any change, and then you have records to give to the hospital, so they can see if there are any patterns that may help figure out what the problem is. In the end, we arrived at the hospital with an unconscious woman, and I learned that when I reach under an unconscious person, I have to be ready for the fact that my hands may get a little messy. Today, it is not an issue, because OSHA (Occupational Safety and Health Administration) required gloves on every call in the early 90s, I believe.

One night, in this middle-class town on eastern Long Island in the mid-1980s, we received a call for a bleeding patient. It was a cool fall night. I ran out to my car and drove to the fire department, which was only about a half mile away. When I arrived and walked inside, I began going through the routine of getting the ambulance ready. First, I hit the button to open the garage door, and then others start arriving. "Yes!" it was a crew of four. It is nice when you actually have what is considered as a full crew. We got into the ambulance and the driver put the sirens on to get to the house. When we arrived at the house, there were cars in the driveway, so we had to park the ambulance in front of the house on the street. I led the crew of four toward the house, and as we got closer and closer to the house, a retched smell got worse and worse. It smelled like a GI (Gastrointestinal) Bleed to me. These are truly the worst-smelling calls an EMT can do. However, this one was even worse than a typical GI Bleed. As I got closer to the house, I heard one of the crew start vomiting behind me. Okay, we are now a crew of three. So, I continued forward, a few steps later, all of a sudden, I heard vomiting in stereo. Another crew member was out of commission for the time being. I kept on moving forward, by the time I got to the door, I realized that I was the only one standing. My last crew member was now on his knees as well. Now to get the true picture of this scene, you must think of the worst smell you have ever smelled and multiply it by ten. You have this two-floor house with a light on at the entrance, at least three cars in the driveway. The house is actually closed, yet the stench is not tolerable. The ambulance all lit up in the street in front of the house and three men scattered on the front lawn vomiting. You never know what will take someone out of commission. Sometimes, it is a smell, other times, it may be the site of the incident or you may know the person such as a family member, or just something that triggered a memory.

Whatever the case, I think every EMT knows that it could happen to them. That is what is nice about having a team, we can all step up for each other if needed. In this case, I needed to get into the house and started walking in, announcing myself as I entered. The smell hit you even harder once I opened the door. I remember telling myself to breath as little as possible. The stairs were nearby and it was obvious to me that the smell was coming from upstairs. So, I held my breath and walked up the stairs. At the top of the stairs, I see a bathroom with the door open, so I walk toward the bathroom and see a middle-aged man sitting on the toilet. I announced myself and asked him what the problem was.

He said, he has diarrhea, and now he is bleeding. I

asked him if he thinks he could walk to the ambulance and he said, "yes," as the bleeding appeared to be minimal at this time. So, he cleaned himself up and got ready to walk with me to the ambulance. Once we got down the stairs and opened the door, there were two police officers standing by the ambulance on the front lawn and by now, the rest of the crew gathered themselves and were standing by the ambulance. Once we stepped outside the rest of the crew came over to help and assisted in getting him into the ambulance. Two of us rode in the back and one stayed up with the driver, as he was still trying to get his composure back. Other than the severe smell, which was mostly trapped in the house this was a basic transport. I am not sure how I made it through this call, but I remember telling myself it was only for a short time and then continued to breath minimally, holding my breath as much as possible while I was inside. I also remember trying to think of positive smells, such as a Christmas tree. Over time, I had learned that a good first step if you know you are entering a GI bleed situation is rubbing Vicks under your nose on your top lip. While I have done many GI bleeds over the years, I do not believe I have ever had a call that smelled as bad as this particular call.

Over the years, I have done a fair number of calls in jails. Calls in jails tend to make you try to be very aware of what is going on. You do not know why they are in jail and you are always wondering if the ambulance is a ploy for them to try to escape. So, the tones came over as a heart patient in the local jail of this middle-class community. I was actually a member of a local volunteer ambulance company in this community and was also a member of the local fire department in my own community. I have some very important rules when I enter a jail cell. The first rule is to make sure that you never have the patient between you and the door or gate. It is a safety precaution but important, because you want to know you can escape quickly if things go wrong. The second rule, is to keep your distance from the inmate, unless you need to touch him or her. I went into the building and walked to the front desk and introduced myself and the officer walked me down to the jail cell. My driver was a little behind as he was positioning the ambulance. The officer opened the gate and let me in.

There was a huge man, probably weighing about 300 pounds but was not that tall, maybe about 5'9." He was standing there, so I introduced myself as an EMT from the ambulance company and asked him what the problem was. He was very talkative and told me that he was having heart palpitations with a little pain. As he is talking, he is moving and using his hands to help his communication, as he moved right, I would move slightly but trying to keep the door nearby. Then he would move the other way and again, like a chess game, I would counter his movement. Now, he seemed like a very nice guy. Although I take that feeling with a grain of salt, again, I do not know why he is where he is. Nonetheless, he explains that he is being studied because he has a very rare heart condition. As he explained and we were playing chess with our positioning, I realized he countered me and that I was now inside with him near the gate and me on the other side. Plus, he outweighs me by about two hundred pounds. I am thinking, "Not good, Jim" "Remember your rule!" So we kept playing chess and I eventually got back to the position I desired. A few minutes later, the guard and my driver came back and joined me. It was actually a routine call with what appeared to be one of the nicest men I have ever met. We talked all the way into the hospital which in this town was only about ten minutes away. Usually when your patient is a prisoner, you have a guard that comes with you. Sometimes, depending on the situation, the police will follow you in case something happens. There weren't any incidents during this call, just my one mistake of positioning.

Back in the late 1980s, in this middle-class community, we received a call for a possible heart attack. When we arrived at this ranch house with a big hardwood front door and a big bay window in the front of the house, we got out of the ambulance, walked up to the door and knocked. A person answered the door and then walked us to the dining room in the back portion of the house. It was being used as a bedroom with a king-size bed in the middle of the room. There was a man lying in the bed who looked like he was in his 30s with short brown hair and probably weighed about 650-750 lbs. There was a strong smell of body odor in the house, as this man likely does not get up often if at all. I introduced myself and asked him, what his name was, he said Harry. Then I asked him what the problem was. He said he was having some minor chest pain and difficulty breathing. So, we carried out a secondary survey and a set of vital signs. His signs and symptoms seem to point toward a possible heart attack.

The problem, in this case, was trying to move him. We did not have any paramedics available and we knew it was going to take time to move him. I called back to dispatch to see if we could get fire rescue sent to the scene with more manpower. When the Chief arrived, I explained to him that we had a 650-750 lb. patient who could not possibly fit through the front door while he was lying down and because he was possibly having a heart attack that trying to have him stand up and walk would be a huge strain on his heart. The only area that I saw that could possibly give him enough space to be taken out of the house was going through the big bay window in front of the house. However, that would call for the removal of that window. Then we had a problem with the stretcher. The stretchers we had, including the actual ambulance stretcher, could not possibly hold the weight and size of this man. So, we decided to take the solid wood front door out and use that as a stretcher. Then it came down to manpower, we decided that we would need at least 12 people to move this man out the window and into the ambulance. Thus, we were short on manpower as well. At the time, we had me, my driver, and five more people, giving us a total of 8. So, the chief had fire rescue start removing the window and called dispatch to bang out more tones for additional manpower. Five minutes later, about five or six firefighters showed up. The rescue company was still working on the window and I was caring for the patient.

I explained to the patient our plan for getting him into the ambulance. The firefighters took off the thick wood front door and brought it into the dining room, where Harry was lying on the hospital-type bed. We removed the covers from the bed and then we had to slowly lift portions of Harry to try to slip the door under him. There was a lot of body to try to navigate in order to get the door underneath him. Once we got the door about halfway under him, we tried to slide it another five or six inches and then started lifting more portions of the fat so we could keep moving the door further and further under him. Usually, you would roll or lift a person and then the stretcher would just slide under, but you could not use that method with Harry, because even if you lifted his skeleton up a foot or two, there would still be a great body on the bed. Fortunately, as this process continued, Harry's good nature helped the situation out. He would joke every once in a while, but you also knew he was scared. He likely had not left the house in years, so the stress of that change in itself would be scary, but then add on being at a hospital for a possible heart attack in the condition he was in, was I am sure it was very stressful. He was also very concerned about whether we would be able to get him to the hospital ambulance. Could we lift him? I explained to him that we have more than enough people to lift him, that we are going to take it just one step at a time and that we will get him into the ambulance. Once we got the door under him, we retrieved straps from the ambulance and two trucks, so we could use multiple straps attached to each other in order to get around his huge body. I believe it took all the straps we had on the ambulance and both fire trucks. The two firefighters came in, telling us the window had been removed and we were ready to start moving him.

The ambulance was backed up on the front lawn as close to the window as possible leaving enough room for firefighters to be able to stand in between the ambulance and the window. So, the plan was to carry him out of the dining room and across the living room and resting the front portion of the door on the frame of the window. This was organized so everyone could pass him hand by hand through the window and into the ambulance. We finished securing the final straps, making sure he was tightly secured to the "door stretcher." The team of firefighters was about ten, so I believe we had four on each side and a couple standing by in case there was a problem. I gave the count, "Okay, everyone on three, one, two, three." We all lifted as a unit and then sidestepped together to get away from the bed. Even with 8 people, this was a struggle and it was good that we had broken this process up into small objectives. Once we got past the bed, we were able to walk toward the window and then then rested the front edge on the window. The front four firemen and the others standing by went outside and got ready for the hand off. They moved quickly to get into position, understanding that you still had four people struggling to hold up the back end of the door.

Once everyone was in position, we began moving the door forward. As the door went through the window, the relieved firefighters would then run outside to get in line between the window and the ambulance. The door was passed hand over hand until we were eventually able to rest it on the floor of the ambulance. It did not sit evenly on the floor because the metal brackets for the actual ambulance stretcher were secured into the floor, but that was actually good because it gave us a few inches under the door to be able to lift it at the hospital. The ambulance, two fire trucks and the chief's car went to the hospital for the next portion of this call. En route to the hospital, I continued to monitor his vitals and gave him oxygen. Because it was a nice day, probably in the 60s, I opened every window I could and turned the fan on in order to alleviate some of the body odor. We arrived at the hospital and got everyone in line to lift Harry out of the ambulance. We had the four on each side and two on the front and back with a couple standing by in case someone needed help and we walked into the hospital with Harry. Harry was conscious, alert and feeling a little less stressed now that he had arrived at the hospital. I am hoping that he had made it through his stay at the hospital and got the help and support he needed to improve his life.

One day, we were called to a house for a possible medical emergency. It was a fairly small house, which when we entered, we noticed that the house was stacked with junk. It was piled everywhere from the floor to about four or six feet high. There was only enough room about two feet wide to pass through these pathways to get around the house. I believe we had a team of four, two EMTs, an attendant and a driver. The wife met us at the door and was emotional and obviously had some psychiatric issues. Walking through this huge pile of junk made you realize that this was a severe hoarder that had lost all control at some point. You had to wonder how it could have gotten so out of control. This place could easily be on the television show "Hoarders." The wife walked us up the stairs and turned left to go down the hallway to the first door on the right, the bathroom. Her husband, a thin man who looked like he was in his late 60s, having a full head of fairly short gray/white hair, was sitting on the toilet. Semi-conscious, as if he was sleeping. My partner and I took vitals and checked his blood sugar level which was very low.

So, I talked to the man trying to see if we could get

a response and he did respond slightly, so I gave him some glucose to raise his blood sugar level, but I was pretty sure he would need more than that to really make the difference so we checked to make sure that ALS (Advanced Life Support) was dispatched.

Bathrooms can be difficult to work in, because they tend to be very small and had a bunch of things you had to work around. Fortunately, the hoarding did not get into the bathroom. Nevertheless, when the medic showed up a few minutes later, we suggested establishing and IV and giving more glucose. I then exited the bathroom because three of us in there at the time was not necessary and I started developing an exit strategy. My partner had already called for backup to help move things to be able to exit because we could not get him out with the two-foot pathway that was there. The wife was very agitated, trying to pace back and forth in between all the junk. At one point, she fell and I asked our attendant to take her into the kitchen, where there was a small space and had her sit down so we did not have a second patient. Not too long later, more manpower showed up and we started clearing a pathway so we could get the stretcher into the patient and the patient out of the house. I believe we chose the stair chair, which is a chair that folds up and has wheels. It is very helpful when you have to go down or up the stairs because it also has a roller on the back of the chair so you can slide it down the stairs. In order to have the space to get the stair chair in and out, we had to clear about 7' in a hallway and then another 4' to the stairs. It does not sound like much, but where do you put it, when the entire place is already piled with junk? So, we added to the height of the existing piles and also found some space in the kitchen. By the time we started moving the patient, the glucose had worked and he was conscious and more alert. Once we got him out of the house and into the ambulance, we had a routine transport to the hospital, with a somewhat normal blood sugar level.

Years ago, I was called to a house on the south shore of Long Island. It was night and we arrived at a well-kept two-story house with an immaculate front lawn. We were greeted at the door by the man's wife. Who brought us to the back of the house where her husband was seizing in the living room. When I approached the patient, he looked like he was in his forties. He was seizing rather violently. When I checked his eyes, one was constricted while the other was dilated. Our job at that point was to protect him from hitting anything and maintaining an airway. We were a BLS unit and we were expecting an ALS unit to arrive. We moved him very quickly using a reeve's stretcher which is great for quick lifts and go. We then placed him on the ambulance stretcher and gave him oxygen. We continued to monitor him as the Medic was just arriving on the scene. The patient continued to seize without a break despite the efforts of the medic. Sometimes you drop a patient off at the hospital, but do not have a good feeling about the overall outcome for the patient. This was definitely one of those times. Obviously, I did not follow up and felt that even if he did survive, he would have lasting effects from this unfortunate medical emergency.

Chapter Ten

Cardiac Arrest

Cardiac arrest is one of the most intense types of calls one can go on. This area of care has changed a great deal over my 42 years. I remember one day in that small beach community that I started in. It was a nice sunny warm weekday; most people were at work. I was home from college. The siren went off and I responded. Since it was during the day, I was the only EMT with a driver. In those days, you did mouth-to-mouth or use an Ambu Bag to breath for the patient. We did not have AEDs (Automated Defibrillation Devices) like we have today. The only thing you could do was CPR. Typically, you do chest compressions in the back of the moving ambulance with people holding your legs so you do not get thrown around with every movement of the ambulance. As we got tired, we would rotate between breathing for the patient, doing chest compressions, and holding the person doing the chest compressions.

Today, we also have machines that can do the

compressions. However, in this case, back in the 80s, I was the sole EMT with one driver and I had to do CPR for forty minutes to the closest hospital, while trying to maintain my balance in the moving ambulance. We transferred the patient to the hospital and we left. I have always assumed he was not saved, but never checked. Again, it is not that I do not care, I was just taught early that you do not take the emotional ride on every call, or I would not last long. Modern-day CPR is much different. AEDs have increased the chance of extending life, providing the AED is on within 3-4 minutes. In addition, the machines that do compressions allow us to have more consistent compressions. You also do not get tired. Sometimes, depending on the jurisdiction, state, and times, paramedics may be able to pronounce or have the MD at medical control pronounce a death while you are at the scene. This cuts down on time spent on patients that cannot be brought back.

Chapter Eleven

Suicides

Over the years, I have gone to many suicides and attempted suicides. In my experience, I can say that men seem to make a decision and end their lives in somewhat of a violent and definite manner. Typically, men use a gun to the head. Sometimes, they use a knife or jump off a bridge or tower. So often, one may walk into a room covered with blood and tissue on the walls and ceilings and find that there is nothing for you to do because the person's head is no longer there or beyond repair. One suicide call stands out to me, perhaps it was because the patient was a male, and we had the possibility of actually saving him. This was a night call when our tones went off as an attempted suicide. When we arrived at the house we knocked at the door, and we were told to go to the bathroom.

The first rule of any scene is to make sure it is safe. During an attempted suicide, it is even more important, thus, when you enter the scene, the first thing you look for is anything that could be used as a weapon, and then you remove it from the scene. So, we walk into the bathroom and we see an unconscious male sitting in the bathtub filled with bloody water. Both wrists were slashed with a razor blade, which was sitting on the window sill next to the tub. We immediately removed the razor and started dressing both wrists. We then put a pressure bandage on each wrist. The patient was unconscious and breathing with a faint pulse. He had lost a lot of blood. In this particular town at this time, they did not have ALS (Advanced Life Support). In other words, there weren't any paramedics. Normally, if you had a paramedic, they could establish an IV to give them fluids to replace the lost blood. Since that was not available, we scooped the man up, put him on the stretcher and went to the nearest hospital. We transferred him to the emergency room alive. I had a good feeling that he likely lived. I hope he got the help needed so he did not finish the job at a later date.

One call I had about 23 years ago came over the pager as a shooting which was not too far from my house.

When you are a volunteer with a pager, the reality is your whole family or anyone who wants to can follow what is going on, because your family will hear the pager and what the call is, while community members may have scanners which are able to pick up the dispatch of calls. So, the pager went off at about 2 AM as a shooting in this calm middle-class neighborhood, the address that was announced was literally around the corner from my home. I got up and started to get dressed when my wife said, "Where are you going?" At this point, I had been an EMT for about twenty years and have dealt with multiple shootings over the years. I looked over to her and said, "we have a call?" Again, she said, "Yes, I know, where are you going?" I said, "I am going on the call." She said, in somewhat of a stern voice, "No, you're not! it is a shooting," I said, "I have been an EMT for many years and have dealt with shooting calls before." I realized at this point she had some concerns, so I felt that I needed to explain my thinking to help her feel more comfortable. So, I said, "Listen, this call is right around the corner and I will not be going directly to the scene until the police say it is secure. But if someone is going to houses and shooting people in our neighborhood, I want to see this person before he/she gets to our house. So, I will be going down the road slightly and just sitting in the car waiting for the police to clear the scene and I will be able to see if anyone is moving towards our house. If they are, they will not make it. So, I then got in my car, rolled down my road slightly without lights and waited for the police to secure the area. Once the police secured the area and they gave the okay to go in, I started my car and went the rest of the way. Unfortunately, it was a suicide that we could not do anything for.

In my experience, women do not usually resort to violence to commit suicide. They also do not often succeed. In fact, almost all the suicides I have gone on for women were intentional overdoses of pharmaceutical drugs like sleeping pills or aspirin etc. These types of calls can be tricky because if the person is not conscious or semi-conscious, finding out what they took and how much maybe difficult. So, unless someone else is there, you have to go by what you see. Perhaps it is an empty bottle of pills in their hand or nearby, or a pill bottle in the drug cabinet which is missing a lot of pills based on the date of the bottle.

Then you have another set of attempted suicides, where they may not have gotten to the point of pulling the trigger, taking the pills or slashing their wrists. And now you show up at the scene for what is referred to as a psychiatric emergency. During all calls, words matter, I learned this as a young EMT when I went to a motor vehicle accident for a woman in her 20s. When I arrived on the scene, she was lying in the parking lot, where she collapsed after getting out of the car. When I was doing the secondary survey on her, it was not uncommon to have to cut the clothes off so you could find and take care of the injuries. This particular day was bright and sunny and as she was lying on the ground, I told her, I have to cut up the side of your leg." OOPS! She started going off, "Why are you cutting my leg? "Once I explained to her that I meant to say "pant leg," she calmed down. That is my one regret that I have had over the 42 years, not choosing the correct words for this young lady. Anyway, during a psychiatric emergency with consideration of suicide, you really need to be on top of your game when talking to the patient. I always try to be positive and try to ask questions that are not directly linked to what is going on, but something that could lead us to a common ground, positive ground or minor negative ground. I know that in some cases, there may not be anything you can say that will change what may happen, but fortunately, I have not seen that yet, or I have totally blocked it out of my memory.

Chapter Twelve
Calls Involving Children

Calls involving children can be some of the toughest calls for EMTs to handle. I remember one call about 37 years ago, where we were called to a house for an infant cardiac arrest. During an infant cardiac arrest you have to move very quickly. We had a crew of four and on our way to the call, we decided that I would be the one to pick up and go. What that meant was that I took the baby, confirmed cardiac arrest and started CPR on the way to the ambulance. The other crew members made sure the path to the ambulance was clear and let me know what to watch for as I was going. Once we got into the ambulance, I placed the infant on the ambulance stretcher and we began to work continuing CPR but changing over to the Ambu Bag for breathing purposes as soon as the baby was secure on the stretcher, the driver was given the okay to go to the hospital.

Fortunately, the hospital in this town is pretty close to our district. However, we had to go through a lot of back roads, twisting and turning, until we got to a main road. "Right turn!" yelled the driver, "Left turn!" "Right turn!" "Right turn!" "Right turn!" "Okay, we are on the main road," all to help us prepare while working on the infant boy. At this point, we had one person doing chest compressions, one person breathing for the baby and one calling the hospital to let them know we were en route with an infant cardiac arrest. We arrived at the hospital about ten minutes later. We dropped off an infant that we tried to bring back, still in cardiac arrest, but shortly after we transferred care, the infant was brought back. There is nothing like a CPR save especially with an infant. You put your heart and soul into it, not expecting any return since reviving someone is a low-percentage task, especially over thirty years ago. By the time we left the hospital, the baby was crying. Then your next thoughts are what happened to the baby, usually at that time, we think it is SID (sudden infant death syndrome). Nevertheless, we got back into the ambulance for the ride back to the fire department. A few weeks later, we were called to the same house for another infant's cardiac arrest. This time, I was driving and we had a full crew of three in the back once again. We went through the same routine and brought the infant to the hospital in cardiac arrest. Again, the infant came back to life shortly after we arrived at the hospital. We could not believe that we had revived the baby now twice. Again, we were wondering what happened, why was this baby going into cardiac arrest? Well, we were happy that the baby was saved and hoping that it was the last time we got called to that house. However, a few weeks later, we were called again to the same location for an infant cardiac arrest. We had the process down and were able to move very quickly and we got the baby to the hospital and again the baby was still in cardiac arrest. Deep inside, we were all hoping that another miracle would happen for a third time. Is it possible to beat the odds three times in a row? Unfortunately, the baby was pronounced dead a little while after we transferred care. We were devastated, angry and wanted answers. Why did this happen three times? What was causing this to happen to this baby boy? We assumed it was SIDs, but often, parents are accused of abuse or neglect when it is actually SIDs. About a month later, we found out that the parents were arrested, but never found out what the outcome was.

Chapter Thirteen
Traumatic Injuries

A ccidents can occur at any time and are always very interesting because you do not know what to expect. Over the years, I noticed trends. There is usually an increase in accidents in and around the holidays, like Christmas and Chanukah. Perhaps it is because I have always been in the northeast and the bad weather contributes, perhaps it is because there are more people on the roads or shopping, or it could be the additional stress the holidays can bring to some people.

One year, I remember being called to a house for an accident with injuries, and when we arrived at this two-story home, we were greeted at the door and told to go to the basement. So, we went down the stairs and there was a man who looked like he was in his forties, he had fairly short black hair and was clean-cut. He was sitting on a couch next to a table saw and was holding a towel over his hand. He was visibly upset. I said, "Hello," and introduced myself as an EMT from the local fire department. I then asked him what the problem was? He replied, "I have been working long hours and I am tired, my wife has been nagging me to fix the manger. So, when I got home, although I should not have worked on it because I am tired, I could not take the nagging anymore, so I tried to work on it. And, I cut off my fucking fingers! Raising his voice and looking upstairs as the final outburst was toward his wife. I then asked him to remove the towel, and sure enough, he was missing three fingers. So, I looked for the digits on the floor around the saw, found them scattered about, then wrapped them up and put them on an ice pack in hoping that the trauma center could put them back on, since this was at a time in the 80's, where we had heard that it could be done successfully. The golden hour is very important here as well. I then dressed and bandaged the wounds and moved him to the ambulance for transport. We brought him and the fingers to the local trauma center. I do not know how he made out at the hospital, but I hoped the surgeons were successfully able to attach the fingers. This call definitely reinforced my thoughts and making sure I do not use power tools when I am tired.

More recently, we had a call at a house where a woman was working on a ladder outside near the garage and fell and hurt her ankle. While we were en route to the call, we were getting the trauma bag set up, thinking we would be using it for a sprained or broken ankle and when we arrived, we found a middle-aged woman in pretty good shape, with blonde hair complaining about her ankle. When we did the secondary assessment, we found a partially amputated ankle, which was actually hanging by some skin tissue and a few blood vessels. It was a clean break and the only thing holding it on the rest of the leg was the little bit of tissue left. You could clearly see the bone end from the leg. Somehow, she did have a distal pulse, which is good news. I took a pillow and actually wrapped everything together since a straight splint was not going to work in this situation. At this point, a paramedic arrived and I told her what we are dealing with and that we needed a line as soon as possible. The paramedic put in an IV, so we were ready to go. The goal at this point was to try to get this person to the hospital without the foot coming completely off. With the golden hour in mind, we loaded her and went to the trauma center. I never heard if the surgery was successful, but I am hoping she has fully recovered.

One day, the siren went off in this middle-class lake community, and it was an ambulance call. I believe it was in the early 1990's. I got in my car, put on my blue light, the flashing hazard lights and started down to the firehouse. It was a nice fall Saturday; the sun was shining and it was fairly warm, probably about 75 degrees. The location of the call was in a residential area. We had a crew of three: a driver, an attendant and myself. When we arrived at the scene of this two-story house with a nice yard, a man met us in the driveway. He said, "I think he broke his leg playing volleyball." He walked us around the house to the backyard. Once we got to the back of the house, we saw a good amount of people having a good time at a barbeque. There was food, drinks, and a good deal of joking around. You can smell the food cooking on the grill. There was a volleyball net set up and sitting up on the ground near the net was a man who looked like he was in his thirties. He had short light brown hair and was in pretty good shape. He was just sitting on the ground alone with a beer in his hand. No one was around, as it seemed they were all having a good time. Occasionally, they would joke around with him, and he would give it right back at them. So, I walked over to him and introduced myself, asking what had happened. He said, "I was playing volleyball and tried to get to the ball and turned too quick and I believe I broke my leg." So, I look down at his left leg and it is obviously deformed at the lower part of the leg, known as the Tib Fib area. I said, "Okay, is it okay if I check you out to make sure there isn't any other injury?" He replied, joking around, "Yes, I have no-where to go." I then asked the attendant to get the Frac Pac out of the ambulance. Frac Pac's are really nice splints with Velcro straps that are designed for each specific body part. The splints are blood-resistant and X-ray-able. Since it was his lower leg, I was thinking that the leg splint would be perfect. I then started the secondary survey to see if there were any other injuries. When you do a secondary survey, you start with the head and palpate each part of the body, working your way down the rest of the body to see if there is any pain, deformity, crepitus, lacerations, abrasions, etc.

While I was doing the secondary survey, I also asked him questions such as, "Do you feel pain here?" "Does this hurt?" "Can you wiggle your toes?" And so on. The attendant came back with the Frac Pac, and I asked him to look for the leg Frac Pac splint. At this point, I started taking his vitals and asking questions about his medical history. Basically, it was exactly what we saw: a deformed lower left leg with no other apparent injuries, and the man did not have any other medical issues. His neurological function was okay but limited on the left leg. It was not a horrible sign but expected. So, at this point, I took the leg splint and slid it from the foot upward to the top of the leg, being careful not to move the leg or cause pain. I then secured the Velcro straps and we placed him on the stretcher. As we were working on this man we can call him Mike, every once in a while, someone would walk up and make fun of the situation.

Mike would just laugh and say something funny in response. Once we loaded him on the stretcher, we started to wheel him toward the ambulance. The people started offering us food and drinks. It was nice to have such a nice sunny fall day, with good people having a good time and keeping a sense of humor about the situation. Of course, we did not take any food or drink, but it was nice to be appreciated for the time we spent away from our own families, who were also enjoying the day without us. We delivered Mike to the hospital in good spirits with a broken leg. We then went back to the firehouse to make sure the ambulance was ready for the next call and then hopefully back to our families to enjoy the rest of the weekend.

PART III UNIQUE EXPERIENCES

Chapter Fourteen

Training and Major Events: Epidemics, Pandemics, and Catastrophic Emergencies

Training

Training is a very important part of being an EMT. It is even more important in areas of a lower volume of calls. Training can occur in many ways. You have certification courses like EMT, CPR, and others, depending on the jurisdiction's laws and regulations. Then you have a recertification course which can be ongoing every few years. You may also have the possibility of testing out every few years, and again, there may be a possibility of earning class credits toward recertification. In addition, every agency will typically do training on such things as driver safety, EMT skills, OSHA guidelines, and much more. As an Emergency Medical Technician, your training never ends. Most trainings are in classrooms, but others can be simulations.

One area of training which can occur on a regular basis but may not be used is that of disaster training simulations. I was very fortunate that while I was attending college in upstate New York, I was flown down to be a triage officer at a major party boat explosion simulation on the Long Island Sound. As a young EMT, I treasured this experience and learned a great deal from it. Most EMTs can go through their whole career and never have this opportunity. As the Triage Officer, I was in charge of the Triage of approximately 65 victims with the following agencies at my disposal: 12 fire department EMTs and ambulance staff, three volunteer ambulance companies, the United States Coast Guard, and the National Guard.

The scenario went like this. There was a boat explosion in the middle of Long Island Sound, and it remained on fire. We sent out a team to go on the boat once the fire was controlled. This team was doing a quick triage assessment and putting patients on boats to come into shore. Because the boat was not stable, the patients had to be moved off the boat as fast as possible. When the patients arrived on shore, they were sent to the triage area.

When we arrived at the scene of the closest shore point from the explosion, the Captain (my mother) identified it as a mass causality incident and established where the triage area would be, the ambulance staging area and the equipment pool. She then appointed crew members to be in charge of the different areas, sending two people out with the Coast Guard to start sending patients in. I was appointed as the Triage Officer at this time. The first few minutes of any mass causality incident is crucial, because it is the organization time that will make or break the operation. Once it is organized, then it is important to have people in charge of each designated area, equipment pool, staging area and triage area. So, as ambulances arrived, they are directed to the equipment pool to drop off all of their mobile equipment, including but not limited to Trauma kits, splints, backboards, scoop stretchers, reeves' stretchers, mast suits, and oxygen. The only thing that stays in the ambulance is the actual ambulance stretcher and extra supplies that may be in the cabinets in each ambulance. Then, the ambulance will drop off the crew to the triage area. Finally, the driver will stay with the ambulance at the staging area, waiting to be called to pick up a patient at the triage area. In the triage area, as each person was brought off the boat and sent to the triage area, I had to assign EMTs to a patient to tag the patient with a high, medium, low priority and/or obviously dead. Then I had to make sure all our high priority patients had EMTs and staff stabilizing them for transport since they were going to be sent out first. Depending on how critical they were, we had a couple of helicopters waiting. Once a patient was stabilized, it was important to assign them to an ambulance or helicopter. The hospital was about 45 minutes away by ambulance, so all of this had to be completed very quickly. Because this peninsula on the north shore of Long Island was so far away from everything, the next closest agency with an ambulance was twenty minutes away and then the trip progressively was longer for all the other agencies. So initially, when we arrived on scene, it was just a couple of us trying to organize everything. It then took about 15 minutes before patients started arriving to the shore.

Once we started receiving patients, the number of patients coming in steadily increased.   Once we started to get ambulances showing up, we had already been tagging and identifying high-priority patients and stabilizing them for the trip. The injuries we were dealing with ranged from simple lacerations and minor burns to major trauma, fractures, head injuries, severe burns to obviously dead. In a perfect world, you would receive them at the triage area in priority order, but since the operation called for quick removal from the exploded boat, they would come in groups with an array of priority levels. In the triage area, we had four designated areas labelled by color. Black was our morgue area for patients who arrived dead, then the red area for critical patients, the yellow area for mid-level priority patients and the green area for our ambulatory patients with minor injuries. It ends rather quickly because everyone is working at a fast pace with the goal of getting the patients to the appropriate hospital as soon as possible.

With any good disaster training drill, there is a full review of the operation, which is very interesting because there are so many pieces and depending on your job responsibilities, you may have only seen one area and did not realize the challenges in all the other areas. Remember, since this was an explosion, there was a whole firematic operation that was carried out as well. So, at this time, all the officers have a chance to speak about their area, what went well, what could be improved and what the challenges were. So, the review gives everyone a full view of the entire operation. After all, it is important to hear about each area because if a disaster occurs, you do not know what your role is going to be. While you cannot totally prepare for all scenarios, you get a chance to see what adaptions had to be made and what were the most important decisions. Moreover, if you are lucky, you may never have to experience a real disaster.

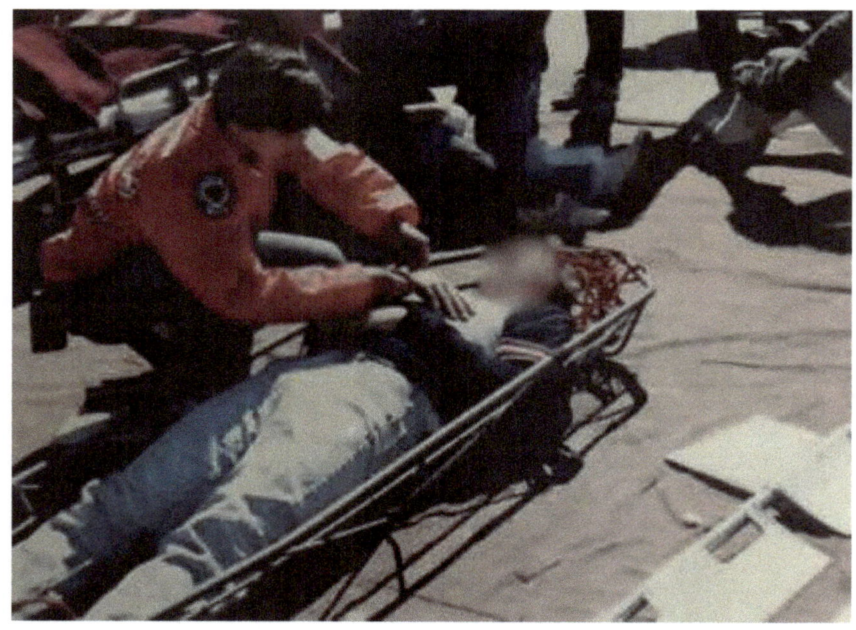

Triage

Triage

Staging area

HIV AIDS

When AIDS (Auto Immune Deficiency Syndrome) hit our country hard, back in the 1980s, it was something that was new and worrisome for first responders. It was at that time when first responders started really making sure they were following protective measures while rendering medical care. It was on the minds of all first responders, at least in the areas I was in at the time. We all learned that wearing gloves and goggles would help limit the possible transmission through fluids. We were also aware of where the potential risks were and how to be very careful when dealing with patients in the high-risk category. So, one of the areas of concern was our drug addiction patients, especially those who were using needles to get their high. We had to be aware of the patient and the needles that could be scattered about or on the person.

Probably the most common issue I heard during this time was when an EMT was accidentally stuck by a needle when caring for a patient. In some cases, needles were used as weapons during a high. It basically changed the way we handled every call and it further prepared us for future incidents. While I did not know any first responders who personally contracted AIDS, I am sure that there are some out there. Fortunately, many of the AIDS patients were upfront and told us that they were infected, so we can make sure we take the precautions seriously. However, there were also some that did just the opposite, spitting at us and acting like they wanted to infect us. These were the ones who were mad at the world.

Perhaps it was just the anger phase as they learned to accept their condition, but it was real and as a first responder that did a fair number of AIDS calls, I did see quite a few that carried on in this manner. Given time in our country, these big threat's, which were very deadly, eventually become a small threat's that can be treated. The health medical care system is always moving forward. Although, one can always criticize the speed at which it moves, when you are reacting to an ever-changing landscape of disease and sickness, I guess there isn't a satisfactory speed. Perhaps one day, we will prevent new sicknesses or diseases altogether.

Ebola

Ebola was probably the scariest possibility for EMTs as it works very quickly and often ends in death. It is because it is so powerful that the transmission does not go too far. People usually die before they can transmit it to other people. While Ebola still surfaces in our areas on occasion, I have yet to come in contact with this disease. Thus, it is one of those things that lurks in the background on every call.

COVID

The COVID-19 Pandemic will be one of the toughest things to write about in this book. Perhaps it is because it is still fresh in my mind and I am still trying to heal from the scars it left behind. It was a very difficult time for first responders and all medical care workers. The risk was high to actually get it and the death rate was also high. In addition, first responders spent their lives trying to save people and did not want to be the ones that brought this virus home or to friends. At the time of the pandemic, I was the oldest and still am the oldest active EMT in our department. I was just under the high-risk category of 60 years old. When COVID came out, it did create an anxious atmosphere which started with a couple of calls and progressed to a point where it was many calls during the day. I remember the first call we received was in a local nursing home. We had training as to how to prepare for the call, so we knew what we had to do. As we pulled up to the facility, I knew we were all nervous. I had everyone suit up for the call and then asked everyone to check each other out to make sure we were all thoroughly protected before went in (picture below).

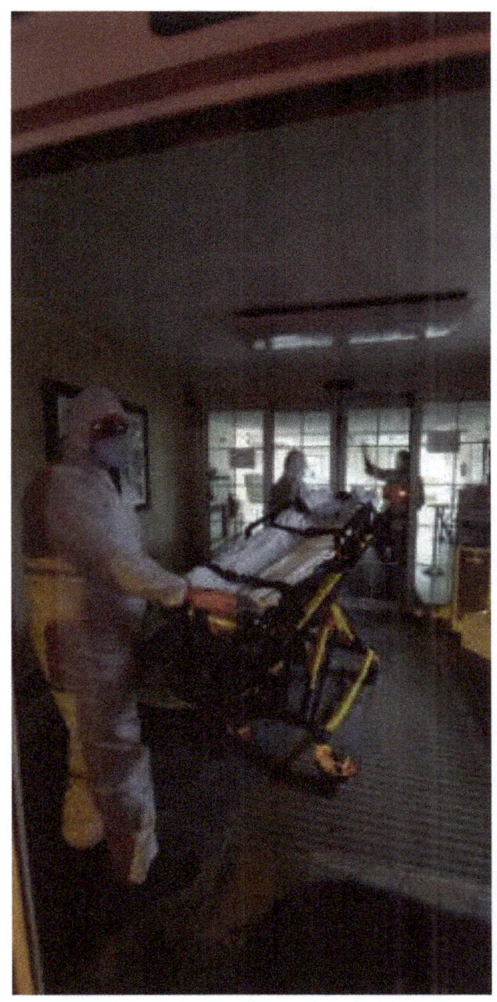

Picture by Dr. Mary Rodda, EMT

This picture was taken as we entered the building. Once we did the call while we were aware of the risks, we were a little more confident that we could handle the calls successfully. I guess we never expected the amount of calls we actually received. It got to the point that New York State changed protocols, having us spend a certain amount of time at a cardiac arrest and if it was not successful, we had to leave the patient behind and move on to the next call. My additional responsibilities were to disinfect the ambulance on a weekday or biweekly basis. What that meant was after every call, we would normally disinfect the ambulance as best as we could by wiping it down and throwing contaminated items away to help stop the spread of this virus. In addition, we purchased a disinfecting lamp which, when placed in the ambulance for a certain period of time, would disinfect the inside even further in case we missed something and to be on the safe side of caution for our patients and our staff. At some point, I remember bringing up the fact that we had EMTs and first responders that had medical issues that put them at a high risk and that they should sit this one out. I believe the recommendation was given to those people by our officers and most of them did sit back, at least for the worst of it. Thus, the result was an increase in call volume and a decrease in manpower, coupled with losing manpower as they contracted the virus. In addition, I had been listed as an essential worker down near New York City and had to go to work daily in a building that had lost life and had a high rate of people that were infected by the virus. So, my day was getting up at 5:10 AM, working and coming home somewhere between 5:30 PM and 9:30 PM, doing ambulance calls sometimes throughout the entire night and coming home and going to work. There were many sleepless nights.

At this point, the loss of life was rising and it was rare if you did not actually know someone that had died. Most people knew many people that had died. My number was seven, there were some people who had much more than that. I believe the most difficult place to work in was in the Intensive care Units in the hospitals. Our Captain of our ambulance was also in charge of the ICU in our hospital and unfortunately, had to deal with death after death. It can be very frustrating when dealing with a new virus and trying everything you can but losing patients anyway.

I remember when the pandemic first hit our area and when I knew what was coming, driving home and making a deal with myself that I would not allow anyone in my house and my work office to die as a result of this virus. I packed my car with a go bag that had clothing and things I would need and told my wife that if I had a bad call where I believed I had a possibility of contracting this virus, I would not be coming home. I had planned on going to a hotel. A bad call to me would have been something where my mask fell off, was pulled off, or something else that made me feel at risk. At my office, I had a meeting with my staff and we took every precaution we could during this time. Because I had a medically fragile staff member and a young woman, it was even more important to make sure that we made it through this ordeal together.

It basically hit the nursing homes hardest, but also did a job on the rest of the population. Since New York City was out of control, we actually had homeless people getting on trains and taking it as far as they could to get away from the death. Often, it would be to our county. While we do not have a train station in my current town, I did multiple calls at train stations in other towns during this time period. During this time, our normal calls dropped slightly since no one was going out and most people were afraid to go to the hospital. Thus, we would often be called to just check out a patient, but then they refused to go to the hospital or we would recommend not going to the hospital if they could wait. The hospitals were overwhelmed with cases and it was a process to just drop off a patient.

Things have settled down considerably during the time I am writing this portion of the book. We are ready to deal with the variants that have come about since the initial breakout, but these variants seem to not be as strong and/or potential victims are much less since the vaccination and death of those from the initial outbreak. Symptoms do not seem to be as severe and therefore, ambulances are not needed as much. I believe most people who have symptoms now go to their doctor or a walk-in clinic.

9/11

September 11, 2001, affected everyone in the world. Whether you were directly impacted by the attacks, knew someone who lost a family member or friend, or watched it repeated over and over again on the television. I still remember putting my kids to bed and explaining to them that the fighter jets roaring across the sky at night were our own and that they were protecting us. I always wondered what affects it had on the children that are now adults. My heart goes out to everyone who suffered a loss that day. Living in the lower part of the state of New York this event had a dramatic impact on me that day, and for months thereafter, while I was attending and watching the many funerals that took place.

I remember that day very well, I was home doing some work around the house, listening to the tones going on calls. I usually do this with the Television on. I then heard the commotion on the television and started viewing all the graphic pictures that started to air. Not too long after I saw that, the tones went off. The resources needed for this type of devastation are enormous. The closer you were to the attack, the closer you got to the center of the attack. Basically, in an event like this you have multiple things going on from a first responders' point of view. First, you have the immediately impacted area, you have many arriving apparatuses and then you try to start bringing in more people who may have been off at the time. Then, since you have drained many other areas, you have to start bringing more first-responding agencies to the areas that were drained and left with no coverage. It is the domino effect; in this case, I believe for the New York area it immediately impacted the surrounding states and counties as resources were called. Then, of course, there was a second wave, once the building collapsed. So, where I was, which was over an hour north of the city, we were called on stand-by to cover multiple agencies that were moved south to cover south of them. Hence, I sat at the firehouse and watched everything going on and answered calls when they came in. Eventually, they changed our stand-by to shifts, until the orders were given to end the stand-bye shifts, which I believe may have been a few days into the disaster. In and around the New York City area, very few people went through this attack without knowing someone who was affected. It was a sad time for our nation. It still makes me worry about the future of our country.

Technology is much further along now, which means militaries have more means to attack further away from their own nation. While we have been attacked on occasion over the years, i.e., 9/11 and Pearl Harbor, I am concerned that the next big war will be fought right here at home, something we have not seen since the Civil War.

Chapter Fifteen
24/7 EMT (On My Own)

As an EMT, I have always taken the responsibility very seriously and have always offered my services in any emergency, provided I felt it was safe to do so. As you read earlier in the book in the Chapter called "First," ever since my first EMT class, emergency situations seem to always appear around me. I know at times, it can frustrate my wife since it has interfered with nights out, parties attended, weddings and many times when we are on the road traveling. Some of this may also be, that I seem to have the ability to see or notice things others just go by. Here are a few examples.

One sunny day, when I was driving down a busy road with water on both sides and a guard rail on my right. I said to myself, did I just pass an unconscious man on the other side of the guardrail? So, I pulled the car over, turned around and drove back to the area. Now, as I go back, I am thinking this is a busy street how can this be possible without others noticing it? When I got back to the area of concern, sure enough, I saw what appeared to be an unconscious male on the other side of the rail. I got out of the car to confirm that he was unconscious and not already deceased. He was a man who possibly could have been homeless or, at the very least, had been having some tough times. His clothes were very old, he had a short beard and it appeared that his hygiene was lacking. I bent over to" Look, Listen and feel," looking at the chest rise, listening for air exchange, and feeling the carotid pulse as well as the air exchange. I confirmed he was alive but unconscious. So, I called 911, and reported the emergency. It happened to be my hometown, so I was able to handle this call from the very beginning until we got him to the local hospital. When dealing with an unconscious person without any sign of injury, it is all about maintaining an airway, making sure the person is breathing and then trying to figure out the reason why he is in this condition. Sometimes, you get to the hospital quickly, depending on the location and situation. Therefore, you arrive before you can get answers. In this case, we delivered an unconscious male to the hospital with stable vitals.

It is funny, just last night on the way home from work, I had a similar experience. I was driving on the interstate going northbound, and the interstate was divided between a median of grass and trees in this particular location. It was a clear but hot summer evening rush hour with cars traveling at about 65-75 miles per hour. It was a wooded area on both sides of the highway. I said to myself, did I just see a black woman standing on the other side of the rail in the woods? I quickly looked around and did not see a broken-down car. There were only woods around, so if there was a person there, then something must be wrong. So, I pulled over and then walked back about 75 yards, and sure enough a black woman and two young children were just standing on the other side of the rail. I walked up to her and said, "Mam, I am an EMT. Are you okay? She looked like she could be in her late fifties or sixties. She had short gray hair and was about 5'2" tall. She appeared to be in shock. She replied, "No, I just had an accident." At that point, I looked over her shoulder and saw a car that was overturned about 75 feet down a cliff in the woods. I asked her, "Is that your car?" She replied, "Yes." I said, "Is there anyone else in it?" She replied, "No." I said, "Is it alright if I check you all out to make sure you do not have any injuries?" She said, "Yes," I told her that I was going to get my bags and equipment and told her to stay on that side of the rail because it was safe there and I would be back in a second. I went to my car, pulled out my gear and then started checking out the victims of this crash. However, I was still puzzled, things did not make sense. The only spot on the guard rail that was dented was about 100 feet in front of my car, yet her car was at least 100 feet in the other direction behind my car. So, while I was checking them out for any injuries, I asked how the accident happened. She said, "I was cut off." Again, things still are not adding up in my mind, we were on the northbound side of the highway and if she had cut off, she would have ended up in front of where I parked. I then asked, "Mam, were you going northbound or southbound? She said, "I was going southbound." So, if what she is saying is true, she was cut off going southbound, lost control, went seventy-five feet down across the median and then seventy-five feet up across the median, was likely air-bound going across three lanes of traffic during rush hour, which was going northbound, did not hit a single car or truck and somehow no one saw this and stopped, she then hit the top of the guardrail then continued another 150' down a cliff before rolling over. Then, she somehow got out of the car, got the kids out of the car and climbed up the cliff to the guardrail. I said, if what you are telling me is accurate, Mam, you and the children are very lucky that you are standing here with no major injuries. At that point, the local fire Chief showed up, and I told him what had happened and he informed me that the ambulance is on the road and should be there soon. A minute later, a fire truck showed up and the Chief had the firemen go down to make sure the car was okay and that there wasn't going to be a fire. A couple of minutes later, the ambulance arrived and I gave them a full report. I finished bandaging the lady and then the paramedic arrived. Once I finished bandaging the lady, I told her she was in good hands now and then departed.

Over the years, I could not even count how many times I had stopped for accidents or other emergencies. One thing is, I never hang around unless asked or if it is a severe emergency and they need my help. You are never sure how different agencies will take the fact that you are there. Do not take me the wrong way, a large majority of the departments I have dealt with are very happy you are there. However, it is always important to remember that it is their department and this is their call. Thus, you do not want to overstay your welcome. Therefore, once the scene is secure and the patients have EMTs attending to them, then I say good bye and move on.

Sometimes, they do not have an EMT coming, and then I may have to go in the ambulance with the patients. This is because in my state, once you render care you can only hand over care to someone of equal certification. An example comes to mind, when we had moved into a new town and a couple of days after we moved, I looked out my window and saw an unconscious male on the road in front of my house. I went out to check the situation and he was unconscious he appeared to be a man in his thirties with short brown hair dressed in jogging shorts and a tee shirt. It was a hot summer day, and once I confirmed that it was an unconscious male who arrived almost at my doorstep, I called 911. Shortly after I heard the sirens go off around the town, a fire Chief arrived. By this time, the man was conscious and talking to me. He had stable vitals and no apparent trauma. The ambulance showed up, but in those days, they did not need an EMT to run an ambulance, so I could not hand the patient over and, as a result, went in the back of the ambulance as the EMT. After the call was over, the Chief drove me home and we started talking, I explained I had just moved into the house a couple of days ago and contacting the fire department for an application was on my list of things to do. Consequently, a few weeks later, I was a member of the local fire department.

Now, I have literally stopped at accidents all over, covering multiple states, and as I said earlier, it is important to make sure that the situation is safe, so you do not get hurt or killed. I remember one time when I was driving home from work and I saw a car a few cars in front of me swerve across two lanes to the left and then swerve back across three lanes to the right. Then, the car went off the road down a hill and into the woods. So, I pulled over. Now, as an EMT, you typically arrive on the scene well after the accident happens, it is much different when you actually see it happen. Hence, once I pull over after seeing something like this, I have to collect myself and prepare to help. I tend to do this by counting to ten to clear my head and then going into action. I then get out, go to my trunk, get my gear, and start heading down the hill into the woods and start working on the patient. She appeared to be in her forties with dark brown hair and definitely had multiple injuries. Of course, I introduced myself and got permission to help her. When I was working on her, I noticed another car pulled over and a man in a brown suit got out of the car and started running over to the accident, as he was running, his jacket flew open and I noticed a gun in his belt. Now, my mind begins to race. What did I get myself into? Was this woman being chased? Am I going to be part of this scene? So, as the man got closer, I stepped away from the car, faced the man and yelled, "Stop right there!!" holding my hands up to stop him. He suddenly Stopped. At this point, he was about 50' away, I then said,

"Are you a police officer?" He replied, "Yes, as he pulled out his badge." I said, "Okay, thanks for stopping and we worked on her for a few minutes until the ambulance arrived.

Sometimes you stop, but there is nothing you can do. One morning, on my way to work in the mid-1990s, I was going southbound down the interstate at about 5:30 AM in the fall. It was just starting to get light out as the sun was rising. A man came running out to the highway, holding his hands up and waving me down. When I pulled the car over and got out, I could see the man was upset. He said to me, He is dead! He is dead! Come with me! So, I followed him down into the trees in the median and there was a car that had run into a thick tree. You can see he was traveling northbound, went off the road traveling in a straight line for about 150' and obviously had it on cruise control because he must have hit the tree going about 65 MPH. He may have fallen asleep, or had a heart attack because there was no sign of trying to slow down. The man who waved me over said I think he was here a long time because the car is cold. So, I checked the engine. It was cold and then I checked the patient, who was also cold, pale had dry blood coming from his mouth and was somewhat rigid without breathing or a pulse. The man had short dark hair probably in his 40s or 50s. This was before airbags were placed in cars. He either died upon impact or was dead from a heart attack prior to impact. Unfortunately, this man, who we later found out was a police officer in the city, was probably coming home from a shift and never had a chance to serve again. I waited for the police to show up, gave my report and then went on to work. This was a tough one to deal with, a fellow first responder was still young and may have had a family. I felt useless, since it was an obvious death, when I got to work, I wrote everything down in case there was a follow-up investigation. I still tear up when thinking about this one, but I understand there are times when you cannot do anything to change the situation.

One time, I was traveling with my family through a congested New York City roadway, and while we were moving very slowly, the car in front of me just stopped. So, I moved into the other lane, passing the car to see if there was anything wrong. I could see a man was very upset, so I pulled in front of the stopped car and got out, the man was yelling, "I think he is seizing or something!" "Help me!" So, I got my bag and told my wife to stay in the car and I will check it out. When I got into the car, the man was having seizures. The man had dark hair, I am not sure of his age, but I was pretty sure that these two men were Italian and had a business nearby, because after I worked on him and put him in the ambulance, the other man gave me his card and said come by anything you want is yours. While my wife and I worked very hard to build a stable life and at times, it was challenging, I never wanted to take advantage of someone in need. I do this as a volunteer to help people and expect nothing. Although, I do appreciate it if someone is appreciative, I never stopped at that business, but I hope the medical condition that this patient had has improved and that he lived a long, healthy life.

On the phone

I often get phone calls from people asking about medical issues and often receive them in times someone is going through an emergency. The emergency calls can come in at any time and are often someone that is not nearby, but knows that I am an EMT. I would not recommend anyone calling an EMT for a real emergency over calling 911. However, in times of crisis, you can expect people to do whatever comes to mind and often, they just need some guidance. One night, or actually early morning after midnight, I think it was about 3:00 AM, I received a call and when I picked up the phone, I heard a lot of commotion, I said, "hello," the person on the other side said there is blood everywhere what do I do? I said, "where is the patient bleeding from?" They started going off about the person falling and rambling on but not really answering the question. I said, "Listen, you need to listen if you want to take care of this situation. "Where is the blood coming from?" He replied, "The head," I said, "Okay" Is there blood anywhere else?" He said I do not think so." I said is the person conscious?" He said, "no" "Did you call 911?" He said, "yes." "Okay, do you have any bandages or towels or something?" He replied, "yes" I said get it and then come back to the phone" I spent the next few minutes talking him through, dressing and bandaging the head of the person who was injured. Eventually, the injured person gained consciousness and then the ambulance arrived. One of the scariest things for most people is when someone is unconscious, they appear to be dead to a person and you can feel useless if they do not wake up. The same problem exists for EMTs. I hate having an unconscious person that you can't wake up. Nevertheless, after about 15 minutes, this emergency was alleviated and, in the end, it was more dramatic than it was a life-threatening situation. After everything settled down, I then said, "Okay, tell me who you are and how you got my phone number?" It turned out it was one of my past college students from many years ago, who remembered, that I was an EMT when the emergency occurred. I do not give my home phone number to students, so my next question was, "Okay, great, how did you get my home phone number?" He said, "I remember the area in which you lived and looked up online and eventually found you." As I said, no one knows how they will act in an emergency and it is even more unpredictable when that person is a loved one. That is true even for EMTs. When an EMT's family member has an emergency, that EMT may not be the EMT they usually are. Other EMTs whom you normally work with will pick up on it even when they may not be aware of your relationship with the patient. I have stepped in on multiple occasions to help a family member of a fellow EMT, And I know they will do the same for me. So, after talking to this caller about things, we said goodbye and the caller went off to the hospital with their family member.

One Sunday at my actual job, where I was the athletic director of this private school, back in the early 1990s, I was just leaving the school building after packing many first aid kits for my coaches. It was a typical summer Sunday at work, I was the only one there because it was the summer and the fall season was starting in a few days. I walked outside toward the parking lot when all of a sudden, I noticed a boy who must have been about 12-14 years old, hobbling toward me, moaning. He was covered with blood and barely able to walk. I called out to him, "Hey, are you ok?" "Do you need help?" He just kept walking. I yelled again, but no response. So, I walked in front of him and said, "Stop!" putting my hands up in front of me. He stopped his hobble. Now that I was closer, I was able to see that he not only had blood all over him, but he was not in good shape, possibly had a head injury and broken bones, had many lacerations and abrasions and his clothes were ripped. I introduced myself as an EMT and asked him if it was okay if I can check him out and help him. He said, "yes." So I told him not to move and quickly went inside, got four first aid kits and called 911. I know he was not one of my students at the school, so I assumed that he must have come from the neighborhood. But I was puzzled as to how this could have happened. I retrieved the first aid kits and came back to the area where the boy was. I asked him his name and he said it was Tom. I told him that I am checking him out to see what injuries he had. My secondary survey showed that he had a possible broken shoulder, two possible broken arms, a possible concussion, multiple lacerations and abrasions. I then asked him how old he was and what had happened, but in his state, he was unable to answer those questions. I started packaging him to stabilize all the injuries. I splinted both arms, put slings and swaths on both arms and dressed and bandaged all the lacerations and abrasions. As I was working on Tom, another boy was coming in my direction on a bike. He was in a hurry and obviously knew something more than I did. I asked the boy, if he knew Tom, and he said, "yes." I said, "Do you know what happened to him?" He said, "yes, we were playing in the back of the school on the basketball courts. He climbed to the top of the basketball hoop and then fell. I got scared because he was not moving, so I ran home and called his mother. His mother is coming." A few minutes later, his mother drives up and is hysterical. By that time, I had him fully packaged and on a longboard, ready for the ambulance. I explained to his mother that I am an EMT and explained everything I found during my survey. I also told her the ambulance should be here soon. She started to calm down, knowing that everything that could be done to help was done. The ambulance showed up about a minute or two later. My athletic department was very well equipped in case we had any major accidents. So, when the ambulance showed up and found a completely packaged child ready for transport with all these injuries, they were shocked. I wiped out four first aid kits on Tom. First aid kits that I had just finished packing for the meeting the following day. Tom had a great deal of injuries with possible internal injuries as well, but I am pretty sure after the casts came off, Tom was back playing again. However, I doubt Tom continued to climb on top of basketball backstops.

About seven years ago, I was driving down to work on a cool fall day, although it was about 5:30 AM and the sun had not come up. Once again, I say to myself, "Did I just see car lights deep into the woods?" So, I pulled my car over, got my equipment and walked back to where I thought I saw the lights. As I got closer, I confirmed that there were actually two cars in the woods. One was about seventy-five yards into the woods, while the second was about a hundred and fifty yards into the woods and overturned. I called 911, reported the accident and then started to approach the first car. As I got near the first car a woman who was possibly in her thirties with medium short brown hair about 6" below the shoulders, who was dressed professionally, was walking toward me. As soon as she notices me, she starts yelling, "That jerk hit me from behind and drove me into the woods because he was racing!" I did not see any noticeable injuries. I introduced myself as an EMT and asked her if she was alright. She stopped for a second to mentally shift from anger to see if she had any pain anywhere and said, "No, but I would like to kill that jerk!" and then changed direction, going toward the other car. I said, "Ma'am, please come with me, it is not safe near the other car." So, I was able to walk her out of the woods and up on the grass near the interstate. As we were walking, I was able to see that her respirations were normal, she had no apparent injury, and she was conscious and alert. So I told her to sit down here and that I needed to check on the driver in the other car. Again, she started screaming, I said, "Ma'am, right now you are okay, the other person may not be okay, please stay here!" I turned around and started walking toward the other car. At this time, I noticed but did not give any concern to a bystander who was standing on the side of the interstate watching this event. As I got closer to the vehicle, I heard it roaring. I noticed that it was a sports car that was upside down with the acceleration still going fast and making a loud noise. I get up to the driver's side window and bend down to see if I could see anything. I saw a silhouette of a person in the car in this very dark wooded area. He appeared to be trying to move, so I tried to open the door, but it was tightly shut. I then stood up, pressed the knob again and really yanked on the doorknob, it moved about an inch or so, good news, it was not locked. Perhaps a little more leverage would help. I then put one foot on the side of the car and pushed with my foot while trying to pull the door open. It was dented, which I am sure made it even more difficult. I got it open about ten more inches. Now I can see that it is a male in his thirties with dark, fairly short hair. I said, trying to be louder than the roaring engine, "Give me a second and I will get you out!" I then put my back on the side of the car, lifted my foot against the inside of the door and pushed the door open with my legs, as the noise of bending metal seemed to be part of this loud scene. It worked enough to get the door open about two feet. I then said, "Sir, turn off the car!" He did. "Okay, now you can come out." He crawled out and was a little shaken up by the accident. Once he got out, he sat near the car and I could hear the woman screaming again in the distance. I then said, now in a normal voice since the engine is off, "Sir, my name is Jim, I am an EMT, are you okay?" Still stunned, the man said, "I think so." I said, "Is it okay if I check you out?" He said, "Yes." I replied, "okay, stay right where you are, do not move and I will start from your head and work my way down your body, you tell me if anything hurts when I touch it." As I started my secondary survey, he said, "I really screwed up, I have to stop this." I said, "What happened?" He replied, "I was racing and weaving in and out and clipped the car in front of me, I am stupid." I said, "yes, but you are also very lucky, you could have killed someone, but at this point, it appears that you are both going to walk away from this with minor injuries." As I continued to work on him, I again noticed this spectator, a man with whiteish short straight hair and black glasses standing on the side of the road. I thought to myself, "he looks awfully familiar." Then the chief of the local fire department arrives and I finish checking the patient. I walked over to the chief and told him he had a two-car accident, both cars in the woods one being overturned. I briefly checked both out and there only appear to be minor injuries. However, due to the mechanism of injury they may need to be checked out at a hospital if they are willing. I also told him that he should make sure they are separated as the woman is very interested in getting a hold of the man. A couple of minutes later, the ambulance arrived and I give the EMT a full report on each patient. I then take my bag and start walking toward my car. I go past the bystander and again, I am thinking, where do I know this person from? I get back into my car and get on with my trip to work. A few days later, I am watching a TV show, and there he is, the bystander with short whiteish hair and black glasses, a famous broadcaster. I knew I had seen him before. I was always wondering what he was thinking as he was watching this incident unfold.

On the way to work about a year ago, I came across an accident in the middle of the interstate. It was two cars, a front and back crash. There was a police officer on the scene, so when I was driving by, I rolled down my window and told him I was an EMT. He said there is one injury that he could use my assistance with, so I pulled over the vehicle and got my gear out of the trunk. When I walked over to the accident scene, the officer said the lady was in that car, pointing in the direction of the crashed vehicle. The others are okay. I walked over to this older, dark-colored four-door sedan, which had a black woman in her thirties with shoulder-length black hair. Her window was down and I could see all sorts of linen and cleaning supplies in the back seat of the car. I introduced myself and asked her if I could help her and she said, "yes." She had a Jamaican accent and she was visibly shaken. I started the secondary survey and asked her what happened and she said, "This white Jeep just came in front of her and intentionally slammed on his brakes." The findings of the secondary showed pain in the neck and the back and small lacerations, but nothing life-threatening. So, I dress and bandage the wounds and then the medic arrives at the scene. I give her my report and then let the medic take over.

I walked over to my car to put my gear away in the trunk, and the officer came over to me and says, "I know you." I said, "well, I drive this interstate every day and stop at accidents, so you likely have seen me in other accidents." I was at the scene for about thirty minutes, got in my car and started toward work. I drove about an eighth of a mile, approaching a no "U-turn" sign and an area for emergency vehicles to turn around, from the opposite direction on the highway, a white jeep pulled in, stopped, and was facing the accident. The jeep stays there for a few seconds, obviously looking at the scene of emergency vehicles. Coincidence? I don't think so, I believe the man was shocked that he caused an accident with his road rage antics and possibly felt guilty and wanted to see how bad it was, or worse, if he came back because he actually enjoyed seeing the lives he possibly changed and the aftermath of his intentional actions. Hopefully, he got caught.

There is an old saying that is kind of a joke in the EMS world. The saying is, "EMTs walk on water, paramedics walk above it." As I have stated in this book on more than one occasion, the people in the EMS world are some of the best people around. However, every so often, you get one that is too good for everyone else. That is why when you are on your own helping out someone, you need to be careful and remember that it is not your call. You are just helping if they want it. One day at work, I went to a cross-country meet for middle school students. It was a big meet in which there was a great deal of schools competing. When I arrived at the school in a neighboring town from where I worked, which is a county south of where I live, multiple people somehow saw me as I walked into the athletic facility. I am known in my work world and hold many leadership positions, as well as being a teacher for coaches' first aid and CPR classes. When I arrived at this school athletic complex, I was above the area of competition and you can see many athletes down on the football field and hundreds of spectators around the area. As soon as I was spotted, I noticed I was being waved onto the competition area, so I walked down the bleachers and onto the field, there was a child lying down on the grass. I asked what happened and they said he just felt weak and had pain in his chest. I asked the young boy, who must have been about 14 years old, if he had any medical history and he said, "No". I took his vitals and he was showing signs of a cardiac episode, which is disturbing for a boy of this age. A few minutes later, I had a full set of vitals and other important information written down on a piece of paper, preparing for the arrival of a paramedic. The paramedic walked up and I introduced myself as an athletic director and EMT. I explained to him that I believed he was having a cardiac episode and gave him the paper with all the information. He took the paper and ripped it into shreds, turned his back to me and started his assessment. This is the perfect example of the saying Paramedics walk above water. He was too good to receive information. The athletic staff standing there were blown away by the disregard for the information. At this point, it was time for me to leave, as the child was under the care of a paid professional who clearly had skills beyond all others. Unfortunately, I had found out later from the coach of the player that the medic did not treat for a cardiac episode and when they arrived at the hospital, the emergency room staff was very upset, as it turned out the child was having a heart attack that was left untreated. Fortunately, he did survive but I was told that the child could no longer play sports.

Chapter Sixteen
Ambulance Incidents

When you ride, as long as I have you are bound to be involved in what can be referred to as an ambulance mishap or incident. This has happened to me about 5-6 times. One call back in the late 1980's, as we got closer to the hospital, I realized that something was wrong, because it got cloudy in the back of the ambulance. Fortunately, the patient did not notice. When I saw this, I stuck my head up to the driver compartment of the ambulance and said that we had smoke filling up the back of the ambulance, the driver said, "we are around the corner from the hospital, we will check when we get there." Once we arrived at the hospital, we pulled the patient out. The driver grabbed the fire extinguisher, we found a fire in one of the outside compartments and the driver extinguished the fire. We found out later that a piece on the exhaust system broke, which created a lot of heat under the cabinet, which in turn started burning the equipment in that compartment.

Ambulance accidents are also something that occurs. I believe I have been in the back of an ambulance three times when the ambulance got into an accident. In all cases, the patient, myself, and everyone else were okay. That is often not the case with ambulance accidents. In fact, just recently, an EMT I occasionally ride with was in an accident where a tractor-trailer hit them and he had to go to the hospital for a large head laceration. Consequently, he is now dealing with post-traumatic stress.

Sleepless Nights

The time I most remember, is when I was in the back of the ambulance in the late 1980's on Long Island. We were coming back to the fire department after a call and we had three of us sitting in the back. One of us started burping, and a couple of minutes later there were two people burping. We did not notice as this came on slowly. When we noticed that two out of three of us in the back were burping, we thought it was funny, but we really did not catch on until I started burping. Now, all three of us were burping. After this, I only remember pieces of what took place. I remember we were laughing in the back of the ambulance because we were all burping. The next thing I remember was being in the Chief's office in the fire department with the three of us literally rolling on the floor laughing and the Chief, our driver, and one other person were just trying to figure out what was going on. The Chief gave the order to take us back to the hospital. I do not remember how we got to the hospital, the next thing I remember was being in the emergency room in our EMT gear, having wheelchair races. If we only had a picture of that, but it was well before everyone having cell phones with cameras. A week later we were told that the county was piloting the use of infused oxygen with nitrous oxide in some ambulances and our ambulance was part of the pilot. However, there was a leak. Nitrous oxide is a laughing gas and is sometimes combined with oxygen. That explains why we could not stop laughing and carried on the way we did.

Chapter Seventeen
The Stories You Hear

This chapter is devoted to EMT stories the author heard from fellow EMTs. I was not witness to most of these calls, and I also have no reason to believe these stories are false, except for how crazy some of them are. Whether you believe them or not, they are entertaining. The first story was told to me by an EMT back in the 1980s. He said he was called out to the motor vehicle accident, and when he arrived at the scene of this two-car crash, he walked up to one car and was astounded to see what he saw. It was two teenagers sitting in the front seat still in the position they were in when the crash happened.

Basically, this young teenager was pleasuring her boyfriend, who was driving at the time of the impact. The problem was that the girl had braces and as a result of the crash, somehow the braces were entangled with the boys' private parts. When I asked the EMT how they handled it? He said like an impaled object. He kept them connected and moved them very carefully to the ambulance, covering them with sheets for privacy purposes. He transported them in the same position, hoping that at the hospital, they could entangle the situation. I hope that the boy did not have any long-term scars from the accident.

The next story is not one that was told to me, but one I actually experienced, but I still find it too crazy to believe. One day, I got a call for an unconscious person on the side of the road. When we arrived, it was a homeless man who was a regular for this department. My partner was a long time EMT for this town and knew the man well. He was also the Lieutenant. For me, it was the first-time meeting "Alex." We arrived at the site and got out of the ambulance and walked up to him and we saw Alex lying on his side unconscious. Alex was about 5'11," had dirty, longer gray hair, a gray untrimmed beard, and was wearing ripped, dirty jeans and a dirty ripped shirt.

We checked his ABC's, and he was breathing and had an okay pulse. We put him on the Pram and into the ambulance. On the ride to the hospital, I took vitals every few minutes, monitoring him to make sure he was okay. On my second set of vitals, he was not breathing and did not have a pulse. I looked over at my partner and said, "I do not have a pulse and he is not breathing." My partner said to try it one more time. So, I tried again and still no breathing or pulse. I said, "no pulse, no breathing, I am going to have to start bagging him and doing CPR." Although, this did not seem to be a bad call, the cardiac arrest did not fit the scenario. My partner said, "Hold on." Then he yelled loudly, "Alex cut the shit!!" and Alex started breathing and had a pulse. Now anyone can hold their breath, but as far as I knew, it was not possible to stop your pulse. My partner looked at me and said, "He has always had full control over his vitals and yet he is homeless, go figure." To this day, I still have trouble believing what I experienced on that call and still question the reality of the situation.

Recently, some fellow EMTs had told me about a call they did where a patient was on the floor in front of a sofa, and when they slid their hands underneath the patient, they realized she was lying in urine and feces. Remember my call many years earlier? Now, at least the EMTs were wearing gloves. This woman was conscious but not really aware of her situation, so now the crew was dealing with the horrible smell of feces and urine, and when they began to move the lady, maggots started coming off of her and they said from within her. So, this scene now has a terrific smell, maggots everywhere, and vomiting first responders. You never know what you are going to walk into, whether it is dangerous, disgusting, or just crazy. You have to be ready for anything. While this call was difficult for those involved, they got the woman to the hospital and hopefully left the maggots at the house. Often, you come to a scene where someone has been there for many hours. In this case, the crew figures that she fell off the couch the day before. Thus, it takes 7-20 hours for maggots to develop, depending on the circumstances, although this crew felt that these maggots may have been there before she actually fell to the floor.

On 9/11, there were many things going on, from the multiple

disaster scenes to the fighter jets screaming across the skies on a regular basis. One EMT had told me that on that day or a day or two after, their ambulance was called to a huge field to pick up someone, from a helicopter. It was a top political leader who was on the move, but the government did not want anyone to know about this politician's movement. In order to move him conspicuously it was done by helicopter and ambulance. I was not told where the politician was delivered to, but I am pretty sure it was not one of our hospitals.

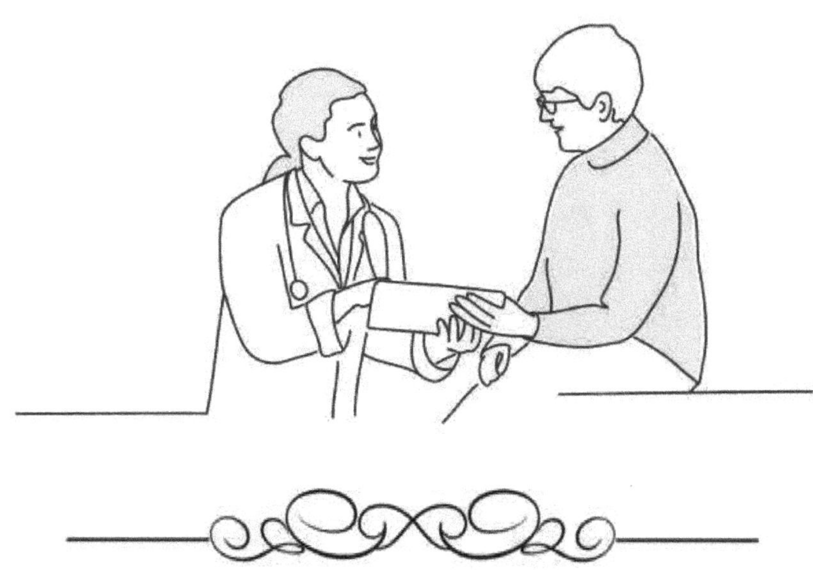

Chapter Eighteen

In Closing

If you google the EMT average career span, it comes up as just five years. This statement is supported by stating it is because of burnout, stress and the physical toll on the body. Being an EMT is not for everyone. Once you start, you will know fairly quickly whether being an emergency medical technician is for you. Often, one can make this decision after a few bad calls. I believe you must have the desire to help others, be able to handle gross and morbid situations, be willing to continuously learn, and have a system in place to emotionally and mentally process everything you experience.

How does one process this type of experience in a healthy way? Each person must have their own way of handling these traumatic events. It is the secret to my longevity as an EMT. The main control that first responders have is being able to not follow up on the outcome of each person they bring to the hospital. One must be disciplined because the emotional roller coaster of becoming emotionally involved with each call will usually end a career. It is not an experience that can be recommended to everyone, it must be a good fit. However, I am always willing to support and mentor anyone who really wants to enter the world of EMS. We have great people! And we need more! Especially towns that have volunteers.

Sleepless Nights

If you want this type of challenge and the feeling that you actually make a difference, remember, this is usually without any recognition or thanks. One must do this from the heart if you want to last. It is a conundrum, you must do it from the heart, but you must protect the heart if you want to last doing it. My first 42 years have passed, and there were times of excitement, enjoyment, high stress, sadness, frustration, anger, and fulfillment. It is an ongoing calling; I am not sure when it will end. But it will be missed when it does. I hope you enjoyed reading just one average person's experiences in the volunteer EMS world. There are many EMTs out there, all doing what they can to help others. Hopefully, you learned a little about what one person may experience as an Emergency Medical Technician. Stay healthy and Safe!